YOUR INTUITIVE GIFTS AT WORK

From Passion to Profession:
The 8 Keys to Excellence in Spiritual Practice

MICHELLE ROBINSON

WHY NOT HAVE MICHELLE ROBINSON AS A GUEST SPEAKER ON YOUR PODCAST, SEMINAR, FESTIVAL OR EVENT?

THE ACADEMY OF SPIRITUAL PRACTICE

Email: michelle@academyofspiritualpractice.com
Website: www.academyofspiritualpractice.com

This is a callout to people with a passion for spiritual development! Michelle Robinson has answered the call to help you propel your intuitive gifts to their highest potential, (in a way that makes you feel safe and supported)

Michelle has 30 years' experience teaching and educating. She is the co-founder and Principal of The Academy of Spiritual Practice. She is a dedicated Mentor to those who feel the 'calling to help others by working with their intuitive gifts.'

You don't need to 'play small.' It is your time to shine

- Michelle cares about helping you feel connected to your soul's purpose.
- She cares about guiding you to excel with your intuitive gifts and reach your potential.
- Michelle cares that you develop self-confidence.
- She is excited for you when you step up to work professionally in Intuitive Practice
- Like any skill, your gifts grow with commitment, training and practice. Michelle says "You deserve to experience that growth for yourself. It's time."

The best way forward is to gather your courage and take the first step. Michelle has a strong professional ethical approach and thirty years' teaching experience.

BOOKS BY MICHELLE ROBINSON

YOUR INTUITIVE GIFTS AT WORK
From Passion to Profession: The 8 Keys to Excellence in Spiritual Practice

Is your soul calling you to step into the power of your intuitive gifts? Are you ready to propel your gifts to their full potential, safely and confidently? Are you ready to stop just practicing your skills and set up a Professional Intuitive Practice? Then this is the book for you.

KARMA COUPLES
A Spiritual Self-Help Guide for Troubled Karmic Relationships

Do you need help to make sense of your romantic relationship? 'Karma Couples' is a self-help book that brings a spiritual perspective to relationships in crisis. It is packed with strategies and meditations to help you assess what your next step might be. A link to 8 free audios is provided in the book.

I'M POSITIVE!
Program Your Thoughts and Feelings to Create a Positive Life.

'I'm Positive!' is your guide to creating an energized, positive life. This book shows you how to steer your life in the right direction. Program your mind so that positive thoughts and feelings are your natural default. A link to 6 free audios is provided in the book.

ONLINE PROGRAM BY MICHELLE ROBINSON
The Certificate in Advanced Intuitive Practice

MENTORING GROUP WITH MICHELLE ROBINSON
Group Mentoring Program for Advanced Intuitive Practice

www.academyofspiritualpractice.com

Download free audio resources
from the author at www.yourintuitivegiftsatwork.com/freeaudios

YOUR INTUITIVE GIFTS AT WORK

From Passion to Profession:
The 8 Keys to Excellence in Spiritual Practice

MICHELLE ROBINSON

Director and Principal – The Academy of Spiritual Practice
B.A., Dip. ED., Bach. Couns., Cert Past Life and Soul Regression, Dip. CH.

"A key has little value, until you put it in a lock and turn it."
Received from Spirit by Michelle Robinson

Brought to you by:
Mind Potential Publishing

Copyright © 2020 Michelle Robinson and the Academy of Spiritual Practice

ALL RIGHTS RESERVED. No part of this book may be reproduced or transmitted in any form whatsoever, electronic, or mechanical, including photocopying, recording, or by any informational storage or retrieval system without the expressed written permission from the author.

Author: Michelle Robinson
Title: Your Intuitive Gifts at Work
ISBN: 978-1-922380-00-5

 A catalogue record for this book is available from the National Library of Australia

Category: SPIRITUALITY/SELF HELP TECHNIQUES

Publisher: Mind Potential Publishing
Division of Mind Design Centre Pty Ltd,
PO Box 6094, Maroochydore BC, Queensland, Australia, 4558.
International Phone: +61 405 138 567
Australia Phone: 1300 664 544
www.thepotentialist.com | www.academyofspiritualpractice.com

Cover design by NGirl Design | www.ngirldesign.com.au

All insights offered are the author's own and are not intended to offend or replace any spiritual beliefs readers may hold. The author respects faith in its many expressions and encourages readers to follow their own beliefs.

LIMITS OF LIABILITY | DISCLAIMER OF WARRANTY: The author and publisher of this book have used their best efforts to prepare this manuscript and they disclaim any warranties, (expressed or implied) for any particular purpose. The information presented in this publication is compiled from sources believed to be accurate at the time of printing and the publisher assumes no responsibility for omissions or errors. The author and publisher shall not be held liable for any loss or other damages, including, but not limited to incidental, consequential, or other. This publication is not intended to replace or substitute medical or professional advice, the author and publisher disclaim any liability, loss or risk incurred as a direct or indirect consequence of the use of any content.

Mind Potential Publishing bears no responsibility for the accuracy of the information provided in online or offline links contained in this publication. The use of links to websites does not constitute an endorsement by the publisher. The publisher assumes no liability for content or opinion expressed by the author.

Printed in Australia

DEDICATION

My book, 'Your Intuitive Gifts At Work' is dedicated to the memory of my friend and mentor Joan Murray.

Joan inspired me with her amazing capacity for love, grace and humor. She was steadfast in her trust in Spirit, a wonderful healer, a spiritualist Reverend and to me, a treasured friend. Joan's gentle and practical wisdom guided me back to my heart, back to my center, back to my soul's calling on many occasions.

Joan never sought the limelight, but rather quietly and competently inspired others by working alongside them. She was courageous, strong and a light in the worlds of many.

I know I am blessed by Joan's presence as she continues to guide me from the spirit world.

Michelle Robinson

"Michelle Robinson has written an indispensable guide to running a successful spiritual practice. She takes the reader on a journey of self-discovery by providing useful insights and sharing stories that are both relatable and practical. If you're running a spiritual practice and want to upskill, read this book and thrive".

Lawrence Taylor Ellyard, Founder of The International Institute for Complementary Therapists
www.myiict.com

CONTENTS

Foreword	1
Introduction	4
Chapter 1: Your Mind Power	13
Chapter 2: Manage Your Energy	31
Chapter 3: Open Your Spiritual Connections	43
Chapter 4: The Essentials of Evidence	59
Chapter 5: Impeccable Communication	81
Chapter 6: The Structure of a Good Session	95
Chapter 7: Looking After You Too	107
Chapter 8: Set Up and Market Your Practice	115
Chapter 9: New Beginnings	137
Acknowledgments	144
Meet the Contributors	145
Further Reading	150
Testimonials	152
About the Author	153
Existing Works by Michelle Robinson	154

FOREWORD

When your soul calls you, it's a message without words, and yet its voice cannot be ignored.

You experience a shift in energy. A heightening of sensitivity. A sense of a greater power guiding your life, and you feel compelled to follow it.

You may be trying hard to fit into the conventional world, succeeding or not, at the roles and challenges life brings you, when, suddenly, you just KNOW that the real purpose of your life is something else. There is a purpose that must be honored, because somehow you know, that's why you are here.

You can no longer hide from the yearning to help others. Your sensitivity opens you to feeling, knowing, sensing the world around you, and it feels like every cell in your body quickens with the realization. The realization that it's time to work with Spirit. It's time to follow your soul's calling.

It's time to work with your Intuitive Gifts.

For some, taking that step can be frightening, fraught with doubt, 'what ifs' and second guessing every decision you make. However, Michelle Robinson's book, *Your Intuitive Gifts at Work*, guides you safely through the transition from doubt to becoming a professional intuitive practitioner. The book provides essential strategies to fine-tune your skills and develop a positive mindset to overcome sabotaging thoughts and support you as you take the next step.

What I most appreciate in this book, is the ethical foundation that underpins every chapter. Michelle's philosophy is that all spiritual work should be undertaken with the intention of healing. Our intuitive gifts are not developed for our ego's sake, but rather to meet our client's needs, to uplift, inspire and comfort those who need our compassion and insights.

So many people in the psychic industry are spiritual seekers, attending workshops, seeking out more training, but never putting what they learn into action. They love practicing their gifts and they want to do more with them, but whether it's self-doubt, not knowing the next best step or even the 'feeling like a fraud' syndrome, there seems to be a stalling point that keeps them attending workshops, wishing and wanting to offer more.

While continuing education is essential and very valuable, many participants also feel dissatisfied that their enthusiasm and learning are not being used at that next level, in professional practice.

> *"Helping you work with your intuitive abilities at that next level, is the focus of this book."*

It reveals the keys to elevate both your confidence and intuitive skills to their highest potential. You will learn how to make the best connections for your work and your client, and, importantly, how to sustain them. If you are a psychic, medium, healer or other allied practitioner, this book provides detailed, logical steps to guide you to set up and market your Intuitive Professional Practice.

With more than thirty years' experience as an international psychic medium and spiritual teacher, I am aware of the need for an honest, grounded approach to living a spiritual life. This is a passion that Michelle and I share.

Michelle's book teaches the importance of self-empowerment and self-responsibility. Managing your own energy is essential. If you struggle with the stimulation in shopping centers or with other people's energies, you will learn how to take control of your energy so other people's energies do not impact you.

I know from my own experience that many clients seek help from a spiritual practitioner when they are experiencing a very difficult period. Often there has been a loss that has devastated their lives. Knowing how to hold a calm yet compassionate space as you work makes you a true professional. In Michelle's book you learn how to communicate with your clients so that you become a messenger of healing and hope.

Michelle and I have shared many experiences over the past twelve years, and I am delighted that this book brings her learning and commitment to Spirit to such a positive fruition. Michelle comes from a compassionate heart and lives in the Light of Spirit.

The spiritual development industry needs a voice like Michelle's that blends our soul's development, our life's lessons and our 'calling' into the development of our unique intuitive gifts to help others in professional practice.

Kathryn Keenan 'Katy-K'

International Psychic Associations 2015 People's Choice Award for Psychic of the Year

Creator of best-selling decks 'The Modern Oracle' and 'The Modern Oracle of Essential Oils'

Director of the 'KTK Spiritual Advancement Academy'

INTRODUCTION

I was first catapulted into the world of spirit in 1994 when I met a ghost in the home my husband and I had recently purchased.

I now know the word 'ghost' was inaccurate, yet back then, I did not know there was a difference between a ghost and a spirit person. Back then, I assumed my house was haunted, and a ghostbuster was required.

You might wonder how I knew there was a 'ghost' occupying my home. The discovery came rather dramatically after joining a meditation class. I had been encouraged by the circle-leader to open my mind and communicate with the spirit world. So, later that night, without any expectations, I lay on my bed, relaxed my body, and asked, *"Hello, is anybody there?"*

I had hoped to connect with my Grandmother, who had died suddenly on the morning of my wedding, but instead, I was shocked to feel strong, warm energy vibrating near my right shoulder. It felt like my whole shoulder was tingling and electric. In my mind, I heard a man's voice saying, *"Don't worry. I won't hurt you."* I sensed his anxiety that I believe him. What was happening? I leaped off the bed and retreated from the bedroom in fear.

Feeling panicked, I immediately phoned my meditation teacher. She used her mediumship gift to tune into my home. Within a few minutes, she reassured me I was communicating with the Spirit of a man who had chosen to stay in the house when he died, rather than move to the spirit world. She clarified a ghost is the energy-echo of a person or event that repeats the same scene over and over. However, a spirit is a living being, like us, in another form. Well, I had a spirit in my home. He was just a man in another form, who meant no harm. In meditation, I began seeing glimpses of a man wearing a pilot's uniform. "Could that be relevant?" I wondered.

Intrigued, I decided to do some research. I was astounded to discover from old newspaper articles that the owner of my home in the early 1960s was a pilot who had died in a light plane crash. He had also flown aircraft during the Korean War, so it was natural that he appeared in a pilot's uniform.

Further inquiries revealed that the people who had sold me the home knew about our 'pilot.' They were unfazed. "*He just does his own thing,*" they said. "*Leave him alone, and you'll both be fine.*"

I can laugh now, but back then, I thought, *"He may be fine, but I am not!"* I swung through a wide range of emotions as I struggled to understand what was happening and what I should do.

- Did he need help?
- Was he 'stuck' here on Earth?
- Should I try to make him leave for the wellbeing of my family?

I was confused, but also amazed. My belief system had been split wide open, and I felt like I was discovering the truth about life for the first time.

I frequently communicated with this Spirit, whose name is Norm. He told me that he had made contact to support me because I had depression. It was true.

In the following weeks, I experienced an enormous amount of learning and emotional turmoil. Although I was not afraid of Norm, I felt his life in our home limited him. About nine months after our first contact, Norm agreed to cross to the spirit world, and that evening my lounge room light spontaneously turned on. A sign to me that he had been received safely on the other side.

For the first time in my life, I believed with certainty in life after death.

INTRODUCTION

I knew that our spiritual essence goes on. My life had purpose and meaning because death was not the end.

I became passionate about developing my spiritual gifts and communicating with those who guided me from the spirit world. My intuition blossomed, and energy streamed from my hands when I meditated.

> For the first time in my life, I believed with certainty in life after death.
>
> I knew that our spiritual essence goes on. My life had purpose and meaning because death was not the end.

After meeting many wonderful people at various stages of exploring their intuitive gifts, I have heard hundreds of individual stories about how people were introduced to Spirit.

I wonder what your defining experience or moment was? The moment or series of moments that caused you to explore your gifts or the meaning of your life?

Perhaps, like me, it was a difficult time like depression or an emotional challenge, during which your spirituality became your way of coping. Maybe you experienced an event or interaction that rocked the previously solid foundations of your life or beliefs. I know I felt that way. Or perhaps, like many people, you have always just known that you were 'different' from members of your family or friends. If you would like to share the story of your introduction to Spirit, feel free to email me and connect. I love hearing about the different ways spiritual journeys evolve. Contact me at michelle@academyofspiritualpractice.com

Although my intuitive gifts unfolded naturally, I had never considered myself *gifted*. I didn't see spirits as a child, and neither did I lie awake at night, sensing ghostly presences in my bedroom.

However, I had always sensed things that many people could not. I was highly sensitive to the emotions around me. If a teacher yelled at another student, I felt both the force of that anger and the student's fear, often as if that fear was my own.

I felt comfortable in some places but overwhelmed in others. Looking back, I felt 'all mixed up' by those places. Talking with adults was often confusing because what they said and did, did not always match what I knew they were thinking.

I sought peace in the quietness of nature and my own company, often wondering why I was not in the body I saw in the mirror. I could separate from my body at will and observe myself in a detached way. Talking with other people always brought me back into my body again, and it became so natural to feel 'in and out' that it didn't worry me. I assumed everyone else felt the same.

Since heightened sensitivity is often the first sign of an intuitive gift, you may feel the emotions of people around you, like I did. Chaotic energies, bright lights, and crowds may make you feel disorientated and off-balance. This book will help you manage your energy so that you do not need to experience that or allow those energies to impact you harmfully. Learning how to remain grounded and centered no matter where you are or who you are with is paramount to working professionally with Spirit.

As I learned more about spirituality and the mysteries of the universe, my spiritual gifts strengthened.

I discovered that, like any skill, practice improved the accuracy of my intuition.

I was not working as a psychic, but psychic gifts, healing energies, and mediumship skills unfolded within me.

During this time, I worked in a mainstream profession as a teacher. I taught teenagers and adults in college.

INTRODUCTION

Beginning gently, I introduced meditation groups twice a week for staff and students and offered free Reiki sessions during the lunch hour on Fridays. In the 1990s, meditation and spiritual healing were not considered mainstream or acceptable as they are today, and so I faced some criticism.

One staff member told me the healing that I believed was coming from a Divine source, was coming from the Devil.

I prayed hard about what that teacher had said. I found the Divine healing energy remained and realized he was just expressing his fears. Those fears had no relevance to me.
I then began teaching spiritual development and Reiki classes at night and on weekends, while still teaching mainstream classes during the week.

All the while, I had unvoiced questions swimming in my mind. My secret doubts about my gifts nibbled at my confidence.

I wondered whether I was really 'good enough' to work professionally with my gifts. *"Would I disappoint my clients or let Spirit down?"* I secretly worried.

More than anything else, I wanted to help people connect to their life's purpose and intuition to help them awaken to the spark of Divinity within them. I wanted them to know that they are guided by loving friends who watch over them in the spirit world. This guidance is only a thought away. Communicating with these spiritual friends is natural.

I had so much knowledge I wanted to share, and yet my fears and doubts were holding me back.

My passion for expanding my knowledge and skills led me to study throughout Australia with leaders in the fields of energy healing, trance, psychic development, and mediumship. For five consecutive years, I attended programs at the *Arthur Findlay College* in England. *Arthur Findlay College* teaches courses that support the spiritualist belief in eternal life and the progression of the human soul. I was keen to enhance my ability to channel wisdom and healing from highly evolved spiritual guides. I wanted to learn as much as I could, so I was a competent and inspirational mentor to others.

As my gifts evolved, the depression disappeared.

I developed a close relationship with the team of spirits who guided me and used my intuitive gifts in my daily life.

I believe every life has a purpose. We come to Earth to learn practical lessons, something that is not so easy in the spirit world where we create with the speed of thought. On Earth, we live with the consequences of our choices and actions. We see how our decisions impact others. Life may be tough at times, but it is all part of our soul's journey.

It was time for me to take a leap of faith.

I completed Counseling and Clinical Hypnotherapy qualifications and bravely stepped into who I truly wanted to be. I set up a professional practice as an Intuitive Counselor and Hypnotherapist. I became accredited in past life and soul regression. I also offered intuitive readings, with a focus on helping clients explore current challenges and move forward.

I kept my work grounded and practical, bringing new levels of understanding, healing, and personal growth to my clients in my clinical practice. I taught workshops to those who wanted to explore their gifts and mentored students as they evolved.

For more than twenty years now, I have guided people like you to develop and work with their intuitive gifts.

If you are passionate about strengthening your gifts and putting them to work, then this book is for you.

You already have knowledge and skills, but how would it feel to lift the standard of your work so that you excelled with confidence

INTRODUCTION

and competence? When you understand how to sustain and use your spiritual connections, the quality of your intuition propels to the highest possible level.

This book teaches eight essential keys to create excellence in your spiritual practice. You have the gifts; now is the time to make them shine.

I work within a highly ethical framework. My wish is that you will benefit from that framework and expand upon the levels of hope and healing that you already offer to your clients. By implementing the 8 Keys in this book, you will strengthen your connections to Spirit, to your gifts, to your clients, and, most importantly, to yourself. You will learn how to step into a confident, professional persona every time you work - a professional persona that feels authentic and just right for you.

The case studies in the book provide real-life examples of how I have been able to help other practitioners who were facing common challenges, though identifying names are changed.

You will also learn the basics of how to set up your professional practice, with practical steps to guide your decision-making, financial research, marketing, and promotion.

You don't have to be psychic, a medium, or a healer to offer clients the benefit of your intuition. Your gifts are who you are. You may currently work in a mainstream role or be a therapist in a complementary healing field like massage, kinesiology, or naturopathy.

> *You may be able to integrate your intuitive gifts into what you already do, offering even more value than before.*

You may already be a psychic, a medium, or an energy healer. It doesn't matter what role you currently hold. Your gifts grow with your willingness to learn, and your empowered intention to help others. Most important is that you use those gifts ethically and wisely. Everyone has a right to privacy.

I provide the 8 Keys to work with your intuitive gifts in a framework of excellence in this book. Whether your goal is to establish a full-time or part-time practice, expand your reach to build a more extensive client base, or develop a reputation for excellence, this book provides the keys. All you need do is integrate these keys with what you already know, and you will unlock the door to your potential.

The first key is all about *YOU!*

Prepare to leave your doubts and limitations behind as you step into the empowerment of all that you are. It is time for some personal alchemy. Your transformation to a confident professional who trusts their gifts begins within. It truly is your time to shine.

Michelle Robinson

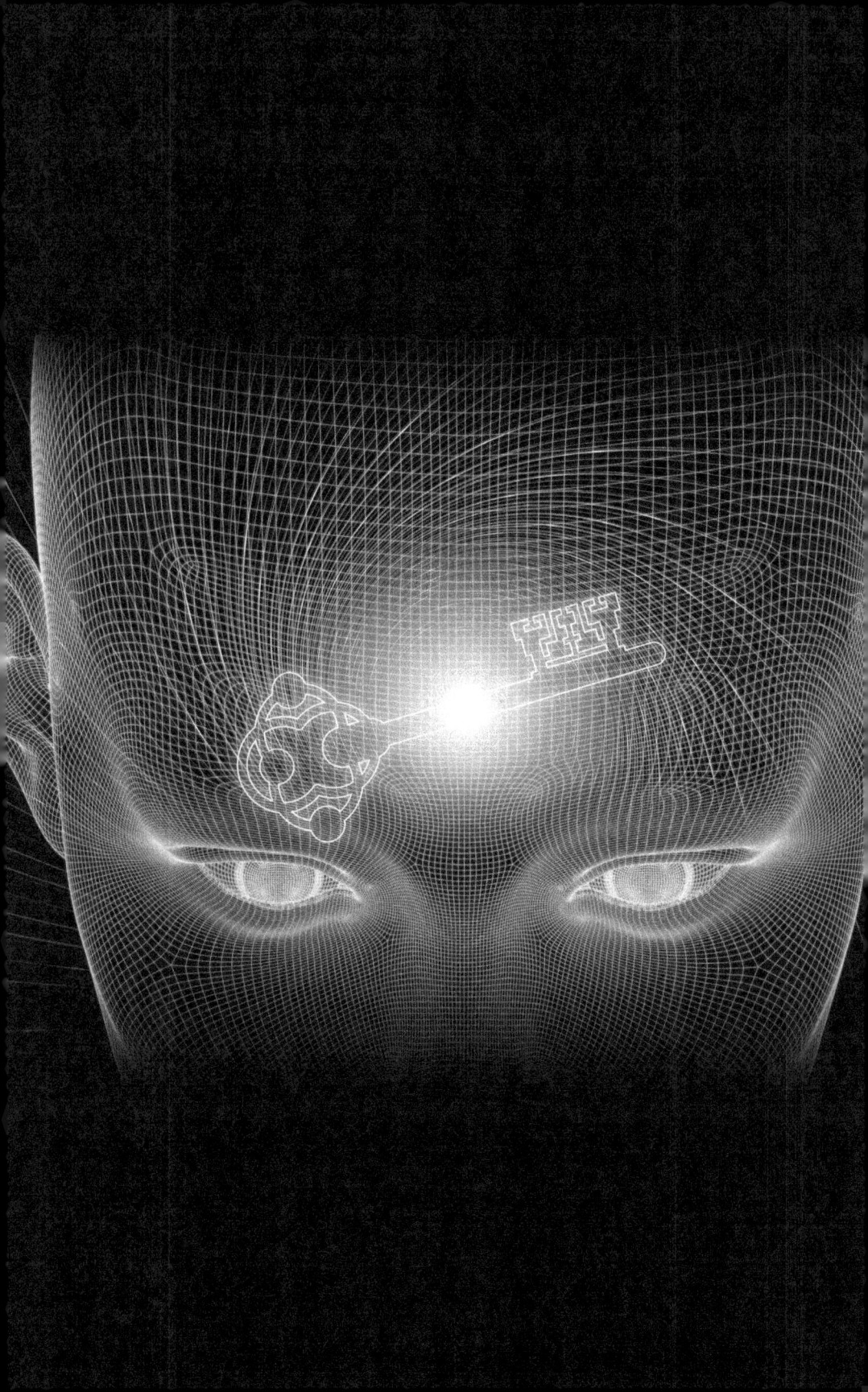

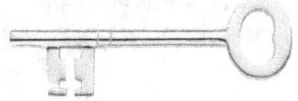

CHAPTER 1

YOUR MIND POWER

Key 1 The Alchemy of Personal Empowerment

The process of alchemy is both exciting and mystical. Alchemists of earlier centuries sought to transform lead into gold, hoping to create power and wealth. The experiments took place in secret laboratories away from public view.

The word alchemy can also describe finding the 'gold' within the human soul through the energy of personal transformation.

When you take the decision to work with your intuitive gifts, you perform your own kind of alchemy - the alchemy of personal empowerment.

All limiting beliefs and fears need to be transformed into a strong self-belief. Only you can do it. When you feel empowered and confident, you strengthen your connection to your gifts.

I vividly remember the first time I offered a psychic reading to a paying client. Previously, I had donated hundreds of readings to friends, family members, colleagues, charity events and the local spiritual church, but had always laughed away suggestions of payment. It was a passion, I told myself. A hobby. I liked helping others. I didn't need payment for that.

One day my phone rang, and a woman who introduced herself as Denise explained that a mutual friend had recommended me to her. She wanted to book an hour's psychic reading as soon as possible and said she would pay whatever I asked.

Self-doubt washed over me like a swiftly flowing tide. My initial reaction was to refuse using any excuse I could. I did not feel prepared mentally or emotionally for a reading to be sprung on me like this. I immediately began to feel like a fraud, the triggers firing in my brain creating all kinds of chaos in my mind and body. However, I had the sense to pause and take a deep breath before I spoke my doubts out loud.

Every day, I worked intuitively with clients in my counseling and hypnosis clinic, helping them find their inner strength. I always lifted my energy, connected with my spiritual guides, and the insights and words the client needed just flowed naturally from my lips.

Every day, my clients performed personal alchemy as they transmuted self-doubt into courage to improve their lives. Every day, I watched in awe as anxious, emotionally vulnerable clients transformed in front of me. They experienced gems of self-awareness that helped them shine like gold as they left my clinic. It was my turn to 'walk my talk', to use the strategies I taught others, and accept the challenge.

I took another deep breath and replied to Denise in a friendly, even voice. *"Of course, let me tell you how I work, and we can see if I am a good fit for what you are looking for."*

After our conversation, Denise was keen to book her appointment and we scheduled the session for late that same afternoon.

All I had to do was transform my emotional butterflies into confident assurance. In doing so, I replaced self-doubt with positive thoughts, set an empowered intention to be of service to Denise, and stepped into the energy of a professional psychic.

The reading was a success.

Since then, I have refined these strategies and now help practitioners from all levels of awareness transform doubts, strengthen confidence and develop their polished, professional persona. This chapter explains the exact steps I took to transform that doubt, so that you may know how to step into your potential too.

The Power of Your Thoughts

In agreeing to Denise's reading, I discovered the power of my thoughts to either help or limit me. At first, my thoughts undermined my confidence, and I faltered. Even though I knew I was competent, I had almost said, "No." Self-sabotaging thoughts nearly stopped me from doing something exciting and positive both for Denise and myself.

> "Yes - I can do this reading. Yes, I have the skills to do it well. I have already helped hundreds of people with my intuition, and yes, I am worthy of being paid for my time."

Fortunately, I caught my thoughts in action and switched them into positive self-talk.

"Yes - I can do this reading. Yes, I have the skills to do it well. I have already helped hundreds of people with my intuition, and yes, I am worthy of being paid for my time."

The energy of my empowered thoughts transformed my nervousness into confidence.

I recognized that my fears were phantoms of the past. I realized that I had always hated letting people down or failing to do something well.

I saw now that my self-doubt was not valid. Fear of failure would not hold me back again.

Your thoughts, whether helpful or limiting, have a huge impact on your intuitive gifts and how you work with them.

Neuroscience tells us that our thoughts create how we experience our reality. Negative and self-critical thoughts are simply neural pathways in our brain that repeatedly fire when triggered by a similar pattern that created them. Each time those neural pathways fire, the same thought is reinforced.

This means that previously limiting choices and beliefs are triggered again on autopilot. When unchecked, critical thoughts or thoughts that trigger you to worry about failure, override the neural pathways of confident, successful thoughts. When this occurs, our confidence is extinguished and the doubtful or critical thoughts 'seem real'. This often leads to a feeling or belief that what we do will never be good enough.

When I think about hesitating over saying 'Yes,' to that first paid reading with Denise, I realize that I had almost fallen victim again to those old neural pathways triggering thoughts of self- doubt. The doubt wasn't actually real today. I felt more confident in my skills. I trusted my intuition. The doubt was simply a phantom of past doubt that was replaying unchecked when the neural pathways fired.

I wonder if you can relate to how I felt that first time with Denise. Can you relate to a time when doubt or fear almost held you back from something you knew you could do?

Sometimes a lack of confidence stems from the past. If you have been bullied or criticized, it takes courage to leave the impact of that treatment behind you. Yet, you can make that choice. You can decide that the past will not rob you of joy in the present.

GAIL'S STORY

CASE STUDY

Gail attended a series of spiritual development workshops I offered because she was keen to extend her intuitive gifts. We discussed common fears and how to transform doubt into confidence.

"It's hard for me," admitted Gail, "because ever since I was a child, I have had a dream of being dragged towards a fire. I wake up with the image of the fire and a crowd of people in front of me. It's terrifying. I even have red marks on my legs that look like flames."

Gail lifted her dress and revealed large red marks that resembled burns covering the lower part of her legs. She had been born with these marks and teased about them when she was younger.

"I am sure I was burned at the stake," Gail added. "My dream is so real."

After hearing about Gail's dream, I was not surprised that she found it hard to trust people. However, she felt compelled to work with her psychic and healing abilities and wanted to feel more confident.

Through energy healing and releasing the trauma of the fire, Gail freed herself from her fears. She recognized that her persecution belonged to the past, and that she could safely use her gifts today.

Perhaps, like Gail, you are aware of something that still impacts you or holds you back. In past centuries, vows of obedience and poverty were frequently made to a church or authority figure. The energy of such vows may still echo in your subconscious memory and auric field.

Payment for your time and skills is a valid and necessary energy exchange. While you may love helping others with your gifts, it is difficult to continue doing so when you cannot fully support yourself financially.

Mind Rehearsal Statements are a great strategy to train your brain to support your intuitive work. These statements become the voice of an inner coach who encourages you to step into your power and fulfill your potential.

The following Mind Rehearsal Statements release blocks to abundance and fears of persecution. Look into a mirror and repeat them as often as needed to clear the energy. You can also create Mind Rehearsal Statements to release blocks that underpin any challenge.

Releasing Blocks to Abundance

In all lives, past, present and future, I destroy all blocks, beliefs and conditioning that prevent me from receiving my rightful abundance. Abundance flows easily and naturally to me. Abundance sustains and nourishes me. I accept my many blessings and am worthy of happiness. So be it and so it is.

Releasing Fear of Persecution

In all lives, past, present and future, where I have been persecuted for my gifts or for being true to who I am, I release this energy and send it to the Source for healing. I am who I am and that is enough. It is safe now, for me to be me. It is safe to use my gifts. All old fear is gone and done. So be it and so it is.

Once you have affirmed your Mind Rehearsal Statements, sense the positive shift that has occurred. You have released unhelpful patterns from the past and welcomed new energy into your life. This change is real. Imagine the new energy expanding as you take deep breaths. Fill yourself with all the good things you have experienced and sense them flowing to every level of your awareness. Consistently choosing to focus on positive thoughts creates new belief systems that open you to new experiences. You will be prepared to say, "Yes," to opportunities the universe presents rather than, "No. I am not ready yet."

One of the most common fears I have helped practitioners overcome is being seen by others as a 'fake' or 'fraud'. Although the practitioner may have intuitive abilities, self-doubt can mean they feel like an imposter. This self-doubt means they tend to 'play small,' restricting how and when they use their gifts. If you or someone you know relates to this, I recommend using the following Mind Rehearsal Statements to boost confidence.

Start by looking at your reflection in the mirror. Next, take a deep breath and connect to yourself as you say:

"Today I will shine. I flow with life. My gifts work naturally and easily."

Place a hand on your heart and repeat:

"Yes - today I will shine. I flow with life. My gifts work naturally and easily."

Tailor these or create your own Mind Rehearsal Statements that resonate with you. Use them every day. Mind Rehearsal Statements are powerful when they are straightforward and easy to remember.

Your Empowered Intention

An empowered intention should be the foundation of all intuitive work.

Your intention is empowered when you infuse your energy, commitment and passion into the outcome you intend. It focuses your purpose and boosts your skills.

When you carry the intention of compassion, all spiritual work is a form of healing.

This is as it should be. Those who guide you in the spirit world know you by your light and are aware of your motivation. They support you in your desire to help others by strengthening your intuition. Your intention is most empowered when it comes from your heart - when you feel compassion for both your client and those in the spirit world you seek to connect with.

Compassion strengthens your connection to your client through your desire to comfort, uplift and offer hope. It is not your role to take responsibility for another person's problems or carry their burdens. You do not help them by denying them the experiences their soul needs in order to grow.

When setting your empowered intention, ask that you are of service to the client according to their highest good or the Divine Plan. Call on your highest spiritual guides, and/or affirm you are a clear true channel for the energy of the Source.

Do not prescribe what the outcome of your work should be. Trust that your best is all that is required.

When setting your intention, be focused, calm and clear. Express yourself in words that feel authentic. You are unique. Honor your abilities.

For example, I compose my intentions in the form of a prayer, but they could be expressed as affirmations or in any form that resonates with you.

Empowered Intention

> ### CASE STUDY
>
> I recently offered trance healing to Chris, who told me he was deeply depressed. My empowered intention was:
>
> *May I be a clear, true channel for compassion, the healing energy of the Source, and the guidance of Spirit. May the Divine Plan for Chris' life be done and may the healing continue after my session with him is over. Thank you.*
>
> This intention could also have begun as an affirmation: *I am a clear, true channel for compassion, the healing energy of the Source, and the guidance of Spirit.*

Your empowered intention does three essential things.

1. It aligns you energetically with what you are about to do. This strengthens your intuition.
2. It connects the client with the highest possible outcome, one that may be beyond your knowing.
3. It lets your spiritual team of guides know that you are ready to work. Provided your intention is positive, they will not let you down. They will assist you to the extent that spiritual and Earthly laws allow.

Remember that we grow as we experience life. Your spiritual guides will not accept responsibility for the decisions that must be made by you or your client.

Set your empowered intention every time you connect with your gifts and the spirit world. Its importance is paramount.

Your Empowered Persona

Creating an empowered persona can be fun. It is your opportunity to become the ideal practitioner. Although it begins in your imagination, with mental rehearsal and a little time, your empowered persona becomes the authentic, new 'you'.

Several years ago, one of my mentors, Lynn, shared her strategy for confidence. As an international medium who works with clients individually and at large events, Lynn needs to keep her energy high.

She creates a positive mindset and maintains a specific wardrobe for when she is working. She even changes her hairstyle and her makeup for work, projecting the persona of a woman who knows exactly what she is doing. Even if she is feeling tired before an event, the moment Lynn steps into her professional persona, it's like putting on a magic cloak. She feels empowered and energized.

Take the time to imagine yourself stepping into the persona of your 'ideal' intuitive practitioner. Imagine:

- What you wear
- How you style your hair
- The colors you choose to represent you
- How your posture, voice and attitude reflect your confidence.

If you are unsure, research top professionals in your field. Watch those you admire on YouTube, read their books or study their work. Notice what you like and do not like about their style and work. Your empowered persona needs to feel just right for you.

Rehearse this confident 'you' every day for at least three months, as this will build the neural pathways to lock in your transformation. What began as ideal, becomes real.

Empower your rehearsal by stepping into a circle of confidence, real or imagined. Strengthen this exercise with a simple affirmation such as, *"Here I am! I'm ready to work."*

Taking a physical step is the most powerful rehearsal method; however, mental rehearsal is also helpful. The more frequently you practice your confident persona and your circle of confidence, the stronger they become. Soon the idea of a projected persona slips away as you naturally integrate your professional behavior into everyday life.

Energetic Protection

The benefits of positive thinking, an empowered intention and a confident persona build a healthy, strong energy field, one that cannot be penetrated by negative thought forms or impacted by other lower energies.

Experts around the world differ about whether you need to ask for protection when working with spiritual gifts. Their opinions reflect their training, the culture of spirituality in their country, their belief systems and experiences.

My experience has shown me that when you think positive thoughts, live a healthy life, and intend to work for the benefit of others, your energy field is strong and impenetrable. Put simply, the power of your positive thoughts and intentions creates the energetic protection you need to work with your spiritual gifts.

I did not know that twenty-five years ago when I lay on my bed and welcomed anyone in the spirit world to join me. Norm meant no harm but opening my energy field so naively was not a wise choice. This principle is easily demonstrated.

> *Treat your energy field like your home. Would you leave it open so just anyone could come in, any time, whether you know them or not? Most likely your answer is 'No.'*

Before I connect with the spirit world, I am clear about my intention. Do I seek personal guidance for a life-issue? Am I preparing to offer healing? Am I reading for a client? Am I sharing spiritual philosophy in trance?

I then 'Sit in the Power' for about fifteen minutes. Sitting in the Power means that you expand the spiritual light within you. This light is known as your 'power'. Sitting in the Power lifts your vibration, connects you to your spiritual essence and prepares you to use your spiritual gifts. Here is how to do it.

Sitting in the Power

Sit in a comfortable yet aligned position. Follow your breath in and out as you allow thoughts to settle.

Rest your focus in the center of your being and imagine a light there. The solar plexus is often regarded as the spiritual center for this purpose. However, it differs between individuals. Many people, including myself, prefer to expand their light from their heart chakra.

Use your imagination to grow that light until it fills your body completely.

Once your body is filled with light, expand your energy until light fills your auric field. Sense yourself sitting in a strong, large bubble of your own spiritual light. This takes only a few seconds once you are experienced.

Sitting in the Power lifts your vibration and makes it easier to connect with Spirit. It also connects you with the energy of your soul.

Next, I lift my energy and invite the spirit world to join me. When seeking guidance, I affirm that only those spirits who love me or work with me as teachers and healers may draw close. When offering healing, I connect directly to the Source - to the Divine

Light - and the healing guides who work with me. I trust that my energy is protected.

Likewise, you should always affirm that only spiritual beings who love you, come from the Light or are your highest guides may work with you.

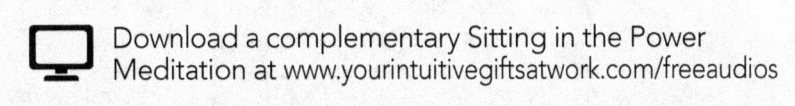
Download a complementary Sitting in the Power Meditation at www.yourintuitivegiftsatwork.com/freeaudios

If positive thoughts and intentions are the foundation of your spiritual practice, you do not need to fear psychic attack or interference from lower astral beings. However, if you worry about someone's negative thoughts, you are more likely to be impacted by them. Similarly, if you struggle with addictions to unhealthy substances or are deeply depressed, you may attract energies who match that lower vibration. An energy clearing session and restoration of emotional and physical wellbeing are your solutions if that occurs.

The secret to your empowerment rests within your mind. My friend, Julie-Ann Bradwyn, is a talented medium. She steps into her confident persona with two simple statements.

"Here I am! Please let me be of service."

She builds her power instantly with the knowledge that expanding her energy is 'just a thought'. She strongly believes that she is always protected by the intelligent spirits who love and work with her. Her positive intention to be of service and her empowered thoughts create a strong energy field. She is never troubled by thoughts of psychic attack or the need for additional protection.

Julie-Ann sets a clear intention, feels her energy rise and is ready to work with her gifts, every time.

When you unlock the potential of your mind, confidence and positivity are the natural outcomes. You perform the alchemy of your own empowerment.

DONNA'S STORY

CASE STUDY

Donna had a problem. Her greatest passion was also her deepest fear. She felt passionate about her intuitive abilities and at the same time, was too afraid to work with them. She lacked the confidence to use her gifts with clients and feared being judged for asking to be paid. *'Perhaps a spiritual gift should not be used to make money?'* she wondered.

Donna's gifts were in great demand with her friends. Since childhood, Donna had noticed she could sense what people were feeling. In her early twenties, she began to know things that were going to happen or what people were about to say. She would get a feeling or have a dream that soon showed up in real life. By the time she was thirty, Donna was sitting in a weekly meditation circle and had completed a course in reading Tarot cards. The story of the cards just seemed to flow, and her friends were shocked at how accurately Donna's insights captured their current challenges. They trusted her gift, but Donna still doubted herself.

Hence her dilemma.

Donna loved offering readings, and since she was working only part-time and had children in primary school, she would benefit from extra income.

I met Donna at a workshop I was teaching on personal empowerment.

She became aware of how her thoughts and self-talk were creating her insecurities. She noticed when she was criticizing herself and changed those thoughts to encouragement with positive Mind Rehearsal Statements.

She reflected on her intentions for working with her intuitive gifts, and realized she genuinely wanted to help people. In meditation, her spiritual guides impressed Donna to understand that even before her birth, her soul had chosen to help others through her gifts.

A big shift came when Donna was able to honor her part in her spiritual development. She recognized that her intuitive gifts were also skills, because she had invested her time, resources and commitment into improving them. Like all skills, they could have remained dormant, but she had chosen to develop them. It was completely valid to use her intuitive skills for her financial support.

Donna found the strength and determination to follow her heart. She learned the power of mind rehearsal and created a persona that transformed her into a competent professional. There was nothing wavering or inconsistent in this new Donna. She chose outfits that reflected her new image. She wanted to feel enveloped in confidence, so a classic style suited her rather than the colorful, flowing style of the stereotyped psychic. She decided to change her hairstyle and wore makeup that projected friendly confidence.

Donna rehearsed this professional version of herself, adding the affirmation, *"Here I am. I'm ready to work!"* as confirmation of her empowered intention.

Word of mouth soon meant that Donna had a thriving part-time business that she could fit in around her other working hours. Financially, she is now more comfortable and has the added satisfaction of working with her intuitive gifts. Her confidence and positive thinking have flowed into all areas of her life, benefiting her in ways she could not have imagined.

Donna's story highlights the importance of using your mind to step into your power.

When you manage your energy efficiently, you never need feel depleted after a long day or overwhelmed in highly stimulating environments. You effortlessly build, sustain and protect your energy in all situations. Excellent energy management is your next key, and one you will find unlocks another door to excellent intuitive practice.

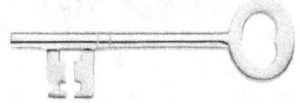

CHAPTER 2
MANAGE YOUR ENERGY

Key 2 Excellent Energy Management

To build the best energy to prepare and then sustain you as you work, more than one approach may be required. You need to understand what works best for you and what type of energy suits your purpose.

> **Krystle's Story**
>
> CASE STUDY
>
> Krystle felt confused. Since experiencing an influx of clients, the quality of her readings had become erratic. When she saw one or two clients a day, she had no problem. If she had four or more clients, she struggled. She was even waking up feeling tired, something that had never happened before. Her nutrition was good, and she slept well.
>
> Krystle began meditating longer before each reading, taking herself to a very calm state. That had worked in the past, but it did not help now.

> The solution to Krystle's challenge was straightforward. She needed to understand her best working vibration so she could sustain her energy during a series of readings. Meditation, which calmed her, did not create the reserves she needed now her practice was busier.
>
> With my guidance, Krystle learned to build her energy before, between and during client sessions. She learned to quickly replenish her energy tank.

Know Your Best Working Vibrations

Like Krystle, you may have experienced fluctuating energy levels or had days when your work seemed easier than others.

Prior to the client arriving, Krystle takes ten minutes to meditate, center her mind and set her intention. It is important to quieten the conscious, analytical part of the mind before intuitive work.

An undisciplined and overactive mind confuses intuitive messages.

After that, Krystle needed to boost her energy. She needed to connect to the spiritual power within her. Listening to uplifting songs combined with some dance movements made her feel alive and vibrant. She imagined breathing in the life-force of nature and expanding her auric field as she sat in her power. This gave her reserves of energy to draw on for multiple clients.

Krystle also discovered that short gaps between readings sustained her energy. Longer breaks just meant she had to lift her energy from scratch again. Twenty minutes between clients, with a slightly longer break for lunch, became her best combination.

In learning how to build and sustain her energies, Krystle's readings regained their quality and consistency.

It is important that you also understand how to build your energy in ways that work best for you. It is not a 'one size fits all' solution. Different gifts require the use of different energies, and different people find different strategies work for them. Excellent energy management places you in your 'zone of best practice'. Knowing how to sustain your power by creating an expanded energy field around you is paramount. This applies whether you work as a psychic, an evidential medium, healer or in another field of spiritual practice.

Evidential Mediums and Psychics

If you are an evidential medium, you connect to persons in the spirit world, providing evidence of the continuance of life after death. You may have seen mediums who work on television such as Tyler Henry or James Van Praagh. Their messages from family and friends in the spirit world offer comfort, healing and closure to those on Earth who grieve.

If you are a psychic, you use your intuition to provide insights about your client's life, their challenges and options going forward. All mediums have psychic abilities and many psychics have some mediumistic gifts. Within one session, the two skills can blend. Perhaps you work psychically, but can also receive messages from loved ones in spirit?

Both psychic work and evidential mediumship, require high energy levels.

Before your client arrives, actively build your energy. Put some extra 'power' in your energy tank.

Tips to Build Energy Levels

- Listen to uplifting music.
- Sing along with your favorite songs.
- Walk, dance, move.
- Imagine breathing in the energies of earth, wave, fire, wind and water.
- Connect with your power and fill your auric field with light.
- Watch something that makes you laugh.

An empowered energy field provides the reserves you need for all kinds of spiritual work.

The only right way is what works best for you.

Trance Mediums

Trance is an altered state of awareness where the conscious, analytical aspect of the mind becomes passive.

A *trance medium* enters a passive state so the spirits who work with them can blend with the medium's energy and mind for purposes like healing, communicating spiritual philosophy, giving evidence of survival after death, writing, art and music. The medium becomes a channel for high spiritual guidance and creativity.

It is important to have a clear intention about the reason you will enter the trance state. The spiritual beings who blend with your energy and impress thoughts on your mind must match your purpose.

It is good spiritual hygiene to be clear and firm about the vibration of the spiritual beings you invite to blend with you.

Remember - you allow them access to your mind and energy to enhance what you do. If the outcome is not higher than what you can achieve alone, then why would you welcome them into your vibration?

It is also important to emphasize that trance guides never enter the body. They blend their minds and energies with the medium in order to inspire, teach and heal, but never to occupy or control. You can insist they leave your energy and thoughts at any time. Trance is a form of mental mediumship because communication occurs through thoughts and feelings.

A *trance healing medium* enters an altered state of consciousness in which their thoughts and body become passive. As this occurs, a powerful energy field builds around them. Their guides use this energy to deliver healing to target the client's specific needs. The medium has no active role except to keep the connection open and be responsive to the level of trance required.

Trance healing is a form of spiritual healing. In trance healing, the blend with Spirit is generally closer than when the medium is consciously involved in the healing process.

Tips to Create Passive Energy for Trance

- Choose a quiet environment where you will not be disturbed.
- Sit in an upright yet comfortable position.
- Relax the physical body and remain still, yet aware of your intention.
- Focus on your breath. Observe or feel it as it enters and leaves your body. Relax deeper with every breath.
- Allow thoughts to pass through your mind. Pay them no attention. Do not judge them.
- Experiment with strategies that guide you to a centered, calm state.

For example:

Imagine coming down a long flight of stairs and relaxing more with every step. Let the image of the stairs fade as your mind settles down.

Fill yourself with a calming color as you follow your breath in and out.

Play music that takes you to a deep state of heightened yet calm awareness.

Spiritual Healing

Most spiritual healers also enter a passive state, allowing the energies of the Source to flow through them with the assistance of their guides. If you are a spiritual healer, you may notice yourself in a detached, trance-like state at times, and feel the energies of your guides blending with yours.

Some spiritual healing modalities require both active and passive energies. You might be active while clearing the chakras and then passive as you channel the energies from the Source. The key to sustaining your energy is to remain aware of where your energy is being drawn from. You need to protect your own energy reserves while at the same time channeling spiritual energy to your client.

Matteo's Story

CASE STUDY

Matteo contacted me because he was feeling tired after his energy healings. He explained that he was a medical intuitive, which meant he sensed his clients' challenges.

Watching Matteo work, I was quickly aware why Matteo was tired.

> Although Matteo opened his sessions by connecting with the Source and the healing guides, he dropped out of these connections as soon as he began discussing his impressions with his clients. Matteo did not realize his healing connection had been lost. He did not re-connect to the Source and within a short while he was sending his clients his own life-force.
>
> I suggested two options to help Matteo stay connected to high spiritual energies and also use his intuitive gifts.
>
> The first option was to begin psychically and deliver his intuitive impressions early in the session. Then Matteo would connect with the Source, keep the channel open and remain silent until the energy waned. He could discuss any additional insights once the healing was complete.
>
> The second option was to delay sharing all intuitive impressions until the end of the session. In that way, the client could relax from the outset.

This straightforward change to Matteo's approach benefited him and his clients. He remained connected to the energy of the Source and no longer drained his life-force. His clients benefited both from his intuitive gifts and the spiritually-guided healing Matteo offered them.

Choose Mindfulness Not Mindful-Mess

I thank Marco Della Valle for introducing me to the concept of 'mindfulness not mindful-mess'. Marco is an international psychic medium, who understands the necessity for a clear mind before he works.

Excellent energy management requires a disciplined mind. A messy, disorganized mind creates interference, like static, in your energy field. It interrupts your intuition and blocks messages from the spirit world. A messy mind also makes it hard to be a clear channel for healing.

I create mindfulness and clear mindful-mess with a straightforward meditation.

You can download it HERE.
www.yourintuitivegiftsatwork.com/freeaudios

Mindfulness Meditation Script

If you would prefer to read the meditation rather than download it, here is a script.

Imagine that you are sitting by the edge of a large lake. The water in this lake reflects how you are feeling. If you are calm and your thoughts are peaceful, then the water is clear, smooth and tranquil. If you feel unhappy, anxious or angry and if your thoughts are chaotic or stressed, then the water is disturbed, muddy and rough.

Take time to sense or see the water in your lake.

Imagine now, that the sun is setting and the energies and colors of a beautiful sunset spill out across the lake and shine right into your heart.

Breathe in the calming colors of gold, pink, purple and blue, and feel yourself settling down. Relax your body, mind and emotions as you rest in the energies of sunset. Use your mind to bring the lake into a peaceful state. See or sense the water become so clear that trees, birds, sky and even your own image reflect on the surface of the lake.

Now you have a clear screen, like a mirror, to receive intuitive impressions and messages.

When you have a calm, inner state, your inner guidance is heightened.

You are also able to discern the difference between what 'belongs to you' and what 'belongs to your client'. It is not helpful to suggest an emotion that is yours is the cause of your client's problems. Mindfulness rather than mindful-mess conserves your energy and creates a clear mental space in which to work.

Manage Your Sensitivity

Do you feel uncomfortable in a world of bright lights, loud sounds, crowds and other people's confused emotions? A heightened level of sensitivity accompanies the unfoldment of spiritual gifts, which can make it difficult to cope.

Perhaps you have very sensitive hearing or an acute sense of smell? You may find shopping centers overwhelming, and you may be aware of other people's feelings, pain and thoughts. This hypersensitivity can leave you feeling drained of energy and emotionally exhausted.

Your sensitivity is both your gift and a challenge. Your senses convey messages from your intuition and from Spirit. However, when you feel swamped with impressions, you probably wish you could turn your sensitivity down.

Fortunately, you can learn to manage your sensitivity so that it works without overwhelming you. With the following energy management strategies, you will be the one in control.

Tips to Manage Energy Sensitivity

- Remember, in the world of adults, you are responsible for only your life. Do not absorb energy that retains the problems of your clients, family or friends. If you have a lot of pain in your energy field and body, release any concerns you are carrying for your clients and those around you.
- Create healthy boundaries. Do not give away your power or freewill when someone else does not approve. Your life is your choice.
- When offering healing, stay connected to the Source and your healing guides. Avoid pouring your life-force energy into the client.
- 'Power down' when you are not working. Do not stay 'switched on' all the time. Relax and live your physical life. You need experiences in the human world for your soul to grow.
- Stay grounded. Re-charge with the energies of nature, laughter, movement and fun.
- Pull your energy field closer to your body. Do this before you go to public places, like shopping centers, or feel swamped by crowds. It only takes an intention and your imagination to bring your energy closer to you. When your energy is expanded, you sense everything. You can also protect your energy with the triple seals of silver, gold and platinum. This prevents unhelpful energies from impacting on you.
- Remain mindful. Do not lose awareness of where you are and dissociate from your body when you are over-stimulated. That causes anxiety and confusion. Retract your energy field, imagine breathing right down to your feet, and relax.
- If necessary, wear ear-plugs, sunglasses and a hat to shelter your most heightened senses. Wearing a covering on your head can protect your crown and mind energy from disturbed vibrations.
- Practice turning down the stimulation in your environment

with the power of your mind. Imagine you have an internal control dial that reduces the intensity of lights, sound, smell, touch and so on. Your belief makes it real. It's self-hypnosis that works.
- Use prayer and a strong intention of protection whenever you need it.
- Remember self-care. When you are exhausted, unwell or stressed, you will be more sensitive. Take time to rejuvenate your energies by Sitting in the Power and doing things you enjoy.

Being sensitive is not an excuse to avoid a full and satisfying life.

Your soul chose 'you' and your life, and so a balance between the physical and spiritual planes is important. Although heightened sensitivity can be challenging, when you learn to manage all aspects of your energy, your sensitivity becomes your greatest gift.

Excellent energy management provides the foundation for the next essential key to working with your intuitive gifts. Your skill in opening your spiritual channels and maintaining strong connections to Spirit and your client plays a huge role in the quality of your work. This is a lock you will want to open. For that, you will become the 'Key Master'.

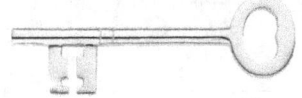

CHAPTER 3

OPEN YOUR SPIRITUAL CONNECTIONS

Key 3 Become 'The Key Master'

Keys can look similar, and yet a lock is opened only with the key that is just right. It's the subtleties of the keys that make all the difference. We've all experienced the frustration of fumbling with a set of keys, unclear which one will release the lock in front of us. Until we select the correct one, the lock remains closed. Whether we want to pass through a door, unlock a treasure chest or open connections to the spirit world, we need the key that works for that intention.

Your intuitive gifts offer you a selection of keys (a range of skills) for your use. It is time now to learn how to open your spiritual channels and create the best connections, every time.

The Art of Blending Energies

All intuitive work involves blending energy to create a connection. You may need to connect with your client, the spirit world and even your own soul. It depends on your intention.

Understanding how to skillfully blend energies and make the right connections for your purpose builds the quality of your work.

Max's Story

CASE STUDY

Max knew his psychic and mediumship readings were adequate, but he felt capable of better. With a background in engineering, Max had a logical mind, and he applied that logic to his readings. If he ticked the mental boxes that represented the topics a client might want to know about, he felt he had done his job. Yet, there was something missing. Max had used this same process for the past two years and nothing had changed. Practice had not lifted the quality of his work.

It didn't take long for me to realize that although Max had natural ability, his approach was formulaic. Max needed to learn how to create an empathetic space for his client.

I guided Max away from the list of topics he usually covered and suggested he tune into the client's greatest need.

Why had the client come to him? What was their deepest need that if it were fulfilled, their lives would be better?

Max learned how to blend his energy with his client by enveloping them in a bubble of respect and compassion. This opened him to a deeper sense of their feelings. As the client's energy relaxed, it became easier for him to connect with their lives.

> Max also learned how to blend more closely with the spirit world. When he became aware of a spirit who wanted to communicate, he invited that spirit to blend with his energy. Focusing on this connection, Max found he became the conduit of love, forgiveness, understanding and healing. His natural gifts finally found their potential. Skillful blending of energies and compassion were the keys that unlocked Max's excellence.

These strategies will work for you, just as they did for Max. When you send your client respect, compassion, love or healing, you create a harmonious blend of energies. This opens your intuitive channels to receive deeper feelings and insights. Everyone benefits.

Knowing how to make the right connection for your purpose greatly enhances the quality of any intuitive work.

The Psychic Connection

Sometimes it is assumed that information is received from the spirit world, when it is the practitioner's own intuitive gifts that provide it. This is frequently the case when a reader or healer is working psychically.

The word 'psychic' derives much of its meaning from the word *psyche*, which relates to the soul, the spirit or mind. A psychic connection connects your spiritual energy to the spiritual energy of your client. At its deepest level, it is soul-to-soul communication.

The psychic link is helpful in many contexts. Here are some examples.

- Tuning into a client during a healing session
- Providing an intuitive reading about a client's life
- Intuitively counseling a client
- Sensing what your child is feeling
- Sensing the cause of your car's problems
- Communicating with your pet

When you work psychically, the client's aura provides much of the information. The connection between you is 'across' from your energy field to theirs.

Unless you connect with your guides and involve them in your readings, psychic work does not involve Spirit. As you tune into your client's soul energy and they relax, their aura opens to you.

The aura is an energy-record of the soul's journey.

It comprises layers of energy, and each layer stores information. When you blend with the client you may sense their events, emotions, relationships, thoughts, hopes, traumas, desires and memories of other lives. Information is received through your channels of extra sensory perception, often referred to as 'the Clairs'. The Clairs include:

- Clairsentience (clear feeling)
- Clairvoyance (clear seeing)
- Clairaudience (clear hearing)
- Claircognizance (clear knowing)
- Clairfactience (clear smelling) and
- Clairgustience (clear tasting)

Clairsentience is usually the first sense to be stimulated. Your clairsentience receives feelings through your solar plexus chakra and transmits information to your other senses. These senses are stimulated to give you additional impressions through sight, sound, smell, knowing, hearing and taste. They provide details that further enrich your impressions.

There is no right order to receive psychic information; different people receive it in different ways. However, your solar plexus chakra, where you experience your emotional responses, is the source of your psychic impressions. You may be familiar with the phrases, *'gut instinct'* or *'I felt in my gut something wasn't right.'*

When you see or sense color in your client's aura you are using clairvoyance. A particular color may mean something to you, but it does not have one, absolute meaning. The same color may be interpreted by another practitioner differently. The auric colors also change depending on which level of the aura you are tuned into, except for the soul colors, which remain largely unchanged in one life. The colors in the emotional and mental auric layers reflect a person's current feelings and thoughts. The spiritual layers reflect levels of spiritual development and may suggest life-lessons and gifts. How the color makes you feel in relation to that client is what counts, rather than the color itself.

Making a Psychic Link

The following strategies encourage a strong psychic link. Experiment with what works best for you.

- Send love, respect and/or compassion to your client, heart to heart.
- Honor the client's inherent Divinity. Affirm to yourself, *"The Divinity in me respects the Divinity in you."*
- Extend your auric bubble around your client so that you embrace them energetically for the period of your work.
- Hold an object the client has brought with them, since this contains their energy. Reading energy in this way is called 'psychometry'.
- Offer a few minutes of healing to your client. There is no need to touch them, but if you both wish it, you might place a hand on their back or shoulders.
- Consider tools such as oracle or tarot cards, photos or a pendulum to link with their energy.

Soul to Soul

For a deeper connection than a standard psychic link, you may connect with your client soul to soul.

Even while we are in human form, our soul is accessible and always attempting communication and guidance. Through establishing a deeper connection with your client, you can tune into your client's soul and provide them with information.

In a soul connection, the aim is to offer healing and upliftment through helpful words.

A soul reading does not provide factual evidence about the client's life, like a standard psychic reading. Rather a soul reading provides gentle wisdom.

The client's soul has a calmer, much less volatile energy than the client's thoughts or emotions. It knows which experiences the client needs for growth and the lessons being learned. When you are calm and connected to your soul energy, soul-to-soul communication occurs.

Connecting Soul to Soul

The following process explains how you might offer a soul reading to your client.

- Extend your auric bubble around your client. Send compassion and love.
- Set your intention to share what the client's soul would like them to know at this time.
- Relax your body, mind and emotions, but remain aware of your client and your surroundings. You may enter a light state of altered awareness, feeling passive and calm.
- Allow your words to flow without editing or analyzing them. If you have a true soul connection, the information you share will be inspired, uplifting and healing.

> Never provide medical advice or any advice that is beyond your professional scope. Do not tell the client what to do, but your words may provide helpful options for them to reflect on.

In a soul reading you may receive information about the client's life-purpose and lessons. The reading may focus on their spiritual or personal gifts and how they can face current challenges. It may include a strategy the client needs for improved wellbeing. It may just feel like you are speaking without really knowing what comes before you say it. If the information is helpful, it will resonate with your client, providing they are open to receiving it.

Never provide medical advice or any advice that is beyond your professional scope. Do not tell the client what to do, but your words may provide helpful options for them to reflect on.

Connections with The Spirit World

The Mediumship Connection

Direct communication with beings who are in the spirit world is known as mediumship.

Connections with the spirit world offer us healing, guidance, wisdom and reassurance of the continuance of life after Earthly death. When you link to spiritual intelligence, your client receives the benefit of information and gifts that are greater than yours alone.

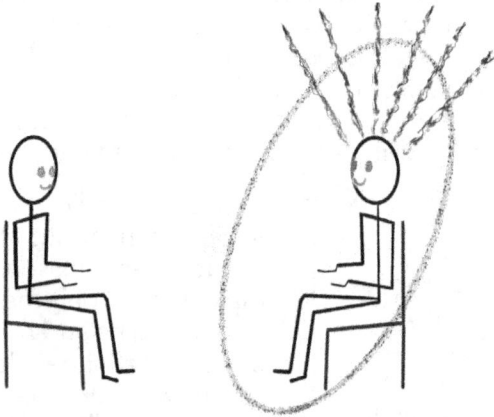

To achieve a mediumship connection, you need to lift your energy up and then out, rather than sending your energy across to your client as you would do in a psychic reading. Your focus is not with the client, but with the spirit communicator who approaches. This is true of both evidential mediumship, which you perform in an aware state, and trance mediumship, during which your mind is held in a passive and subdued state by your spiritual trance guides.

If you blend with the client without lifting your focus to the spirit world, you encourage a psychic link and may not create the vibration for mediumship.

Tips for Establishing an Evidential Mediumship Connection

- Build your energy first. Sit in the Power and expand your aura.
- Set a strong intention to be of service to Spirit and your client. Come from love and compassion first and always. Love connects the human and spiritual worlds.
- Lift your energy beyond your aura, with the intention of linking to a spiritual communicator. Stay focused.
- Consider a wide variety of possible spirit communicators. Open your mind to mothers, fathers, sons, daughters, friends, grandparents, pets and all other relationships. The spirit contact your client expects may not be the one who is able to communicate.
- Encourage the approaching spirit communicator to blend with your energy.
- Remain highly aware of what you experience with all senses.
- Stay flexible and change gears when appropriate. During a psychic reading, you may sense the presence of a spirit person approaching. Lift your energy and focus on them to receive their message.

The Trance Mediumship Connection

The central aspect of trance mediumship is that the medium's mind becomes passive so that their spiritual communicator has a level of hold over the medium's mind.

> *This does not mean that Spirit 'takes over' the mind, but rather the mind is held in a quiet state so that Spirit may use the medium as their channel for healing, inspiration, evidence and creativity.*

When bringing philosophy through trance, one spiritual guide may represent the wisdom and energies of a team who blend with a medium. On other occasions, such as when bringing survival evidence, one spirit may work with the medium at a time. The term 'trance-control' or 'spirit-control' is used to describe the spirit who communicates or leads the interaction during trance.

Trance alters like a dimmer switch. It's not just 'on' or 'off'. The levels of spiritual trance blend gently like the colors of a rainbow. The closer that Spirit draws to your physical body, the deeper the blend of energies. A harmony between Spirit and the medium is essential - there are no random members of a trance-team. Dedication and time are required.

Tips for Establishing a Trance Connection

- Have a clear intention for your trance. The level of trance depends on your purpose.
- Ensure you are in an environment where you will not be disturbed by phones or interruptions. You will be in a highly sensitive state.
- Lift your energy to meet your spiritual team or communicator and then surrender. Quieten your mind. You can't make trance happen through willpower.
- Request that Spirit take you to the level of awareness you need to be. If you try to control your depth, you may not

be in the best state for connection to flow. Deeper is not always better, especially if you become so passive you cannot speak, write or paint.
- A harmonious blend creates a smooth trance experience. Any feelings such as a pressure or tightening around your chest and head signal you are still harmonizing your energies with your spirit-control.

You will naturally emerge from trance when the time required is over. You always have a level of awareness. Even if you fall asleep, you will naturally waken.

Features of Trance

At least twenty minutes may be required for you to blend effectively with your trance team. Do not rush your connection or its deepening. You may experience some, or all, of the following features while you are in trance.

- A deep inner stillness and feeling of wellbeing
- A pale complexion and shallow, slow, calm breathing
- An increased heart-rate, which soon settles
- An awareness of another energy, or perhaps other thoughts or impressions, moving into your mind. This is called being 'overshadowed' by Spirit.
- Temperature changes around you as your body responds to the new spiritual energy in your auric field
- Temporary tightness around the back of your neck and throat as your energies blend with your team
- A sense of drifting, floating, being 'far away'

An experienced trance medium may blend so closely with the energy of the spirit-control that the control enters into the role of the medium. It is the control's personality, rather than the medium's, that communicates the information.

This deep blending allows the medium to take on the same gestures, intonation, words and mannerisms of the spirit-control. It takes a high degree of rapport between the personality of the medium and the personality of the spirit-control to achieve this state and relay accurate evidence. *Sunny Burgess*, from Australia, is an excellent trance medium who brings stunning evidence from communicators through his spirit-control in the trance state.

Connection with Spiritual Guides

Like every soul on Earth, you have a team of spiritual helpers who guide you. Those who assist with your gifts will change as your needs evolve, yet all have a positive intention. Your spiritual guides protect, teach, inspire and offer healing, according to your soul's lessons for incarnating in this life. They communicate through your thoughts and imagination, using your frames of reference.

You may be aware of one guide more than others; however, this guide is usually the communicator for your team.

Tips for Linking with Your Guides

- Establish a clear intention for the connection. This intention determines which spiritual guides will join you.
- Sit in the Power for a few minutes, and then lift your energy and focus higher, beyond your aura. Invite your spiritual

guides to draw closer to you.
- Keep your appointments with your spiritual friends. Be reliable and committed.
- Connect on some occasions without expectation. Just send your guides gratitude for their support.
- Always thank your guides for spending time with you.
- Appreciate your gifts and stay open to learning. Unfoldment takes time. When you honor yourself and your gifts, you also honor your spiritual teachers.
- Be ethical and honest. Do not claim everything you say and feel is channeled from your guides. A close relationship with your teaching guides requires high levels of integrity.

The Spiritual Healing Connection

Healing is the core intention of all spiritual work. Energy healing can be offered whether the person is present with you or not, and you may choose to have physical contact with your client or not.

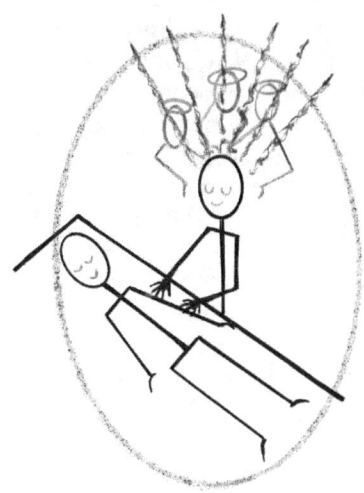

It is not the purpose of this book to teach you how to offer spiritual healing as there are hundreds of different modalities.

Regardless of your preferred modality, your energy connection needs to be effective.

Tips for Linking to Spiritual Healing Energies

- Clear and center your mind and your emotions. Expand your energy field by Sitting in the Power and/or breathing in the energies of nature. A strong energy field helps bridge the gap between the human and spiritual worlds.
- Set a clear and compassionate intention. Ask to be a clear, true channel for the healing energies of the Source, according to the Divine Plan/highest good for your client.
- Lift your energies to connect to the Source. Request your spiritual healing guides to assist.
- In trance healing, lift your energy towards the Source, then become passive and ask your spiritual team to take you to the best level of awareness for the work that needs to be done. This level may change during the healing.
- Maintain focus. Do not become distracted. If you lose the connection, always re-connect.
- Trust the process. Your healing guides work with your energy in multiple ways, depending on the need of the client. The energy flows wherever it is needed.
- Give thanks when the healing is complete. Like hanging up a phone, disconnect and then release all responsibility for the outcome. Clear the energies in your environment and ground yourself with food, a drink of water or physical activity.

Master Your Keys

Your gifts are multifaceted. Being proficient in blending energies and transitioning connections supports excellent intuitive work.

Within a single session your gifts may vary. Sometimes, a psychic reading or a healing morphs into mediumship. You may receive information about the client from your intuition and then become aware that a person in the spirit world is impressing memories in your mind. You lift your energy and focus on the spirit contact, and suddenly you are working in a mediumship vibration. Your client receives a heart-felt connection from someone who loves them, and this is healing for your client and also the spirit communicator.

Your competence in blending energies and opening the appropriate spiritual connections is essential in your intuitive work. These skills underpin the next key to excellence - a key that determines whether your client leaves your session as a fan or a critic.

What do your clients want when they book an intuitive session?

They want to feel that you understand their needs and their unique issues. They also want you to prove that beyond what they now experience, there is 'more'. This 'more' offers you the space to create your magic. You have the opportunity to show your clients the reality of life after death, the mystery of the psychic senses and the strength to carry on during times of struggle. What do your clients really want?

Your clients want you to provide them with high quality evidence. In the next chapter I will delve deeply into the importance of high-quality evidence, what it is and how to ensure you provide it.

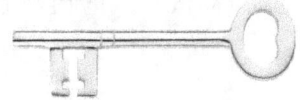

CHAPTER 4
THE ESSENTIALS OF EVIDENCE

Key 4 Provide High Quality Evidence

The information you provide in a psychic or mediumship reading is called evidence. The quality of that evidence will determine how your client remembers you.

If you provide accurate, helpful information, then they will become your fan. If the evidence is vague and irrelevant, they will remember little else.

This chapter will show you how to extend your personal evidence database and demonstrate high quality evidence in psychic work and mediumship.

Build A Symbolic Database

Your life's experiences build the database that constructs your evidence, and this database is accessed by both your intuitive senses and your spirit communicators. An extensive personal database is invaluable in your work, since it is difficult to receive an impression about something you do not understand.

I discovered this first-hand. I was unfamiliar with the sport, gridiron, which was my client's passion. I knew he loved a particular sport, and it was similar to football, but I had no clue what to call it.

My database let me down because I had taken little interest in sport. I had gaps in key experiences that were routinely required when providing evidence.

Once your database sends you an image, the challenge is to work out whether that image is literal or needs interpretation.

In a psychic reading with Dianne some years ago, I saw gelato in a cone and heard 'gelato' in my mind. Rather than passing on what I received, I tried to interpret it. That was my mistake.

"*I sense you enjoy Italian cooking,*" I ventured.

"*No, not really,*" replied Dianne.

"*Perhaps you are traveling to Italy?*" I continued, still looking for something to talk about involving gelato.

"*No,*" she replied looking puzzled.

Finally, common-sense prevailed. "*I see gelato,*" I said, feeling a little exasperated with myself.

Dianne burst into laughter. "*Oh yes,*" she replied. "*It's my favorite dessert. I made my husband take me to the gelato shop last weekend for our anniversary, and I had three different flavors in the one cone. He teased me about it all afternoon.*"

I laughed as well, which broke the ice and helped us relax. However, it taught me that passing on what I sense is the best way to give evidence. If the client does not understand it, then interpretation is the next step.

Your database gives you clues about your client using your frames of reference. You may clairvoyantly see a wedding you attended which represents a wedding coming up for a client. A relative from your life, like an aunt, may be shown to represent an aunt in your client's life. A symbol you understand, such as a green light for 'yes', may be shown when the answer to the client's question is yes. This is how your database works and a comprehensive database is a wonderful resource.

Strategies for Extending Your Symbolic Database

- Mentally catalogue significant memories from your life. Include holidays, weddings, funerals, birthdays, anniversaries, promotions, home buying and selling, graduations, children's milestones, traveling overseas, winning awards, illnesses and so on.
- Be observant. Notice the symbols on signs around you. Observe stop signs, give way signs, detours, road closures, hazards, traffic lights, roundabouts.
- Notice parks, sporting grounds, hospitals, schools, colleges, daycare centers, police stations, swimming pools, ambulance stations, hotels, shopping centers, public toilets.
- Create a relationship list. Select your mother, father, partner, siblings, child, a friend, grandparents, cousins, uncle, aunt, pets and so on, to represent that relationship in your symbolic database. You may be shown one of 'your people' to illustrate that relationship for your client.
- Be curious beyond your own experiences. Watch TV shows about different cultures, food, travel, current events and sport. Be interested in the world and people. Family members and friends who are now in the spirit world lived real lives. They did not just sit around looking at crystals and meditating. They need real-life experiences to draw on in your database.
- Create a dictionary of important symbols. Here are several symbols from my database.

> A green light symbolizes 'Yes. Go ahead.'
>
> A red light symbolizes 'No. Stop.'
>
> A cake with candles symbolizes a birthday.
>
> A bunch of flowers symbolizes an anniversary.
>
> A storm brewing shows me there's trouble ahead.

Make sure the symbols you choose are clear and consistent.

Using Oracle Cards in Your Symbolic Database

Learning the images and meanings from a deck of oracle cards is a very effective way to build a symbolic database. It is one of my favorite strategies to receive a quick psychic message for myself or a client. I find *The Modern Oracle* by Katy-K works well for this purpose because the images and meanings in the deck are straightforward and clear.

Firstly, I decide the number of cards required to provide my message. I usually choose between one and three cards. Next, I mentally toss the complete deck into the air, imagining the cards landing on a table. In my imagination, the cards that land face-up correspond with the number of cards I have chosen for the reading. These cards provide my message. All this occurs in just a few moments. It is a handy strategy to receive a psychic message because the strategy is portable. You can use it anywhere, any time. You can also use any deck that is easy to remember and feels comfortable for you.

The Nature of Evidence in a Psychic Message

Psychic evidence relates to your client's life. In most cases, it is based on what is currently occurring or has already occurred.

While it is possible to see some future scenarios, the impressions you receive may be possibilities rather than fact. A change in the client's actions may change their future.

It is very important to remember that psychic information, in most cases, is not predictive.

For prediction you need the presence of Spirit, and even then, what is shown is restricted to what is beneficial for the person to know. Many experiences the soul needs must occur in the moment and without preparation.

Making an assumption that psychic information predicts the future, presents risks for the client.

Imagine that I clairvoyantly see my client at university.

I say, "*Wow. You are going to university next year.*"

My client responds, "*Great! I have just been thinking about that! I never thought I would get there! I didn't think my grades were good enough. What a relief!*"

If I am tuned into my client's energy field, I may have read what my client wants, not what will happen. The risk is that they will stop their hard work and assume they will gain entry to university without lifting their grades.

It would have been more responsible to have said, "*I sense university study around you. Can you relate to that?*"

If my client confirms they have been thinking about it, I would use my intuitive gifts to help them explore how they might achieve their goal.

I could also ask for insights from my guides. If knowing a future event is beneficial to the client, the information may be made available.

Imagine the damage a psychic could do if they predicted a marriage break-up that a client had been lightly considering but had never planned to action. Doubt could be sowed that caused real harm.

The key to providing excellent psychic evidence is to address the client's reason for seeing you. Check if the client has a preferred focus or question of importance. It is too late when the reading is over to discover their needs were not met.

Explain that what you receive may not match what they hoped to hear, but you will be honest. Make no guarantees. Their human wants and soul's needs may differ.

The following topics are often addressed in a psychic reading.

- Family
- Career
- Relationships
- Travel
- Hobbies
- Finances
- Home life
- Study
- Spiritual and personal development
- General health and wellbeing

In sharing your impressions about these subjects, always help the client explore possible options.

Never give advice, especially in health, legal or financial matters. Remind the client that they are responsible for their decisions.

Expanding Psychic Evidence with Tools

The choice of whether to use tools to build evidence in a psychic reading, is yours.

Photos may also link you with significant people or pets in the client's life. To save any embarrassment, confirm if the person or animal in the photo is still living.

Connect with the person or animal through their eyes and aura. If the soul refuses permission for you to read them, you will feel blocked; this is not your failure. They have a right to their privacy. Be gentle in your messages. Never slander or frighten someone based on what you sense in a photo.

Using Cards as a Guidance Tool

Do you have a favorite deck of oracle or tarot cards? You will find some decks 'feel right' and others do not appeal.

Your spiritual guidance may even lead you to a particular deck.

Recently, I had a dream where one of my teachers from the *Arthur Findlay College* gave me a bunch of roses. One was deep red, and the others were pink and white. He told me that I had important work to do. When I awoke, this seemed no more than a strange dream.

The next morning, I was browsing in a crystal shop. A deck of cards lay on the counter, face-up. I drew 2 cards and the essence of their messages was:

You have been training for centuries for this.

You are a teacher - how will you lead?

When I turned the cards over, I discovered the back of every card was covered in red, pink and white roses.

Because I resonated with the deck, I bought it, but I also knew I had been guided to hear that message.

If you use cards, then looking after them and attuning to them before you begin a reading is important. Kathryn (Kath) Simeon is a professional psychic medium with a very large fan base due to the detail and accuracy she provides in her psychic readings.

Kath's Tips for Connecting with Your Cards

Kath often uses cards as a connection-tool. She shares her tips for attuning to a deck of cards in preparation for a reading.

- "Before buying a deck of cards, be sure you truly resonate with them. Your relationship with the cards is vitally important.
- Wrap your cards in silk to protect their energies.
- Center yourself with a short meditation and prayer before the client arrives. Ask that the universal energies assist the person you are reading for. The universal energies may be your guides or whatever higher wisdom you believe in.
- Ask the client to shuffle the cards as they think of the issues they would like clarified during the reading.
- Tune into what the cards suggest for that client and let the cards stimulate your psychic senses. Let your intuition guide you.
- When the reading has finished, clear the cards' energies and remember to express gratitude for your guidance."

As Kath reveals, it is important to tune in to what the cards suggest about your client. The same cards will provide different messages on different occasions. Use your intuition to interpret the symbols, pictures, words, colors, movement, patterns and relationship to other cards. Let the cards 'talk' to you about your client's life and feelings. Where are your eyes drawn? What feels significant?

It is important to set a clear intention before you begin.

The intention, *'Let's do a spread that explores your current work situation,'* is very different from, *'Let's do a spread that explores what might happen if you changed jobs.'*

Your intention guides your interpretation. If the intention is not clear, the messages will be vague.

Take control of the reading. Choose the layout and how many cards will be read. Decide who selects the cards and where they are placed. If you are connected to your client and your intention is clear, your cards strengthen your evidence.

In summary, high quality psychic evidence:

- Demonstrates an understanding of key issues and challenges in the client's life
- Provides relevant, accurate information
- Helps the client explore options and possibilities
- Is communicated with empathy and respect
- Empowers the client to make their own decisions.

The Nature of Evidence in Evidential Mediumship

The aim of evidential mediumship is to provide proof of life after death. Messages from loved ones in spirit inspire us to live with resilience and courage.

If you promote yourself as a medium, you indicate you can communicate with the spirit world. Evidential mediums communicate with spirit persons who are known and recognized by the client.

An effective medium conveys credible evidence that identifies the spirit communicator to the client.

Credible Evidence in Evidential Mediumship

Credible evidence is information that the client understands and accepts about the spirit-communicator. A blend of the following information builds a strong evidential message.

- Factual information that is verified by the client

For example: the spirit communicator's name, relationship to the client, cause of death, places lived, career, hobbies, family members, age when they passed, birth month, shared memories with the client, heirlooms that belonged to the spirit person, significant events in the client's life that have been witnessed since the spirit communicator crossed to the spirit world

- Information that is convincing but less factual

For example: the spirit person's character, habits, beliefs, behaviors, relationships with other family members

- Information that cannot be proven but is still believable based on what is known

For example: who met them when they crossed to the spirit world, what their life lessons were, what they are learning now, what their environment is like in the spirit world

- Information that is an extension of what is already known

For example: "Your mother loved growing roses on Earth and is continuing to garden in the spirit world."

Poor Evidence in Evidential Mediumship

Sometimes the link with the spirit world is not clear and the evidence is unconvincing.

Poor evidence:

- Feels out of character, does not fit with what is already known, is very general and/or does not establish the spirit communicator to the client

- Contains personal bias by the medium
- Frightens or depresses the client rather than uplifts, helps and heals
- Is exaggerated with unprovable claims such as, "Your mum is reincarnating as a Lama in Tibet."

How Do You Receive Messages in Evidential Mediumship?

Your Senses

Your heightened sensory channels of feeling, seeing, hearing, taste, smell and 'knowing' are your highways to communication. They work for you in psychic and mediumship readings, except in mediumship, a spirit contact uses them to provide you with evidence about their life.

You may sense, see, know, hear, smell and even taste impressions from the person in spirit. If they smoked, you may smell and taste tobacco. If they loved cooking Italian food, you may smell the pasta sauce, taste garlic and see them, in your mind's eye, in the kitchen.

Most clairvoyant and clairaudient information will be received subjectively. This means you see images and hear voices in your mind rather than seeing images and hearing voices outside of your mind.

Personal Clues

Stay aware of what you notice about your client. You may be drawn to earrings or a watch that belonged to or was a gift from the spirit. The color of your client's eyes or their name may feel as though they have importance.

You may realize a song is playing in your mind. Listen to the words and share them. That song may be significant.

I recently heard the song, '*Tie a yellow ribbon round the old oak tree*,' during a reading. My client, Sue, tearfully explained that she had always tied a yellow ribbon around a tree in the front yard to welcome her husband home when he worked away. It was almost the ten-year anniversary of Bruce's death. The song was an important clue that Bruce had come to communicate with Sue.

Your Personal Database

Your personal database is extremely helpful in mediumship.

You may receive a flash of someone you know to give you a clue about the spirit person. It might be the relationship to the client, the name, their personality or how they died.

You may receive memories of events from your life that are relevant, such as a trip to Paris.

Let Spirit Guide You

The best way to gather evidence is to let the spirit communicator guide it. Do not bombard them with questions you want answered such as, "How did you die?" Many spirits want to be remembered only for how they lived. While it is important to establish the spirit's identity with some facts, it is also important to bring to life their essence and their character.

> While it is important to establish the spirit's identity with some facts, it is also important to bring to life their essence and their character.

Would a father in spirit who is desperate to communicate with his grieving daughter most want to say, "I had brown hair and was average height," or "I felt you holding my hand when I passed. I have never left you."?

The mediumship connection requires significant energy. Allow the spirit contact to use their limited time with their loved one to share their most important messages.

> *Gather enough facts that the client identifies the spirit person and then let the spirit share what they choose. You are the conduit, not the conductor of the message.*

The communication skills of both the spirit contact and the medium affect the success of the interaction.

Sometimes one spirit will pass on messages on behalf of another who is still learning how to connect with loved ones on Earth. This often occurs if the spirit is that of a young baby or child.

Because the vibration of Spirit is much faster and higher than our own, it can be difficult to hear messages accurately. All the medium's senses, not just hearing, are important in building accurate evidence. If you are developing mediumship skills, train yourself to notice everything you experience through your senses, even while you are not working.

Dealing with Multiple Contacts

Be aware that one spirit person often brings in other spirits, so keep your mind open to multiple contacts. This is understandable, since families and friends are keen to re-connect when the chance is offered. Sorting out messages from more than one spirit person takes experience.

> *Sometimes you need to acknowledge and then 'park' a second spirit, promising to return to them when you have finished with the first.*

You can minimize the confusion by clearly asking for one spirit contact at a time. Also ask for someone who is known and recognized. If a great, great grandmother comes forward, it is unlikely the client will be able to verify information about the grandmother's life. Someone from a closer generation could provide more relevant evidence.

You also need to let the client know that you cannot control who comes through. The client may not receive the contact they expected.

One of the best readings I have experienced began with my Siamese cat, Chloe. Her appearance was very unexpected, but she was the first spirit to appear to the medium, and Chloe identified herself by her name. Soon afterwards my mother followed. My Mum had only passed a few months earlier and Chloe opened the connection for her. The reading was excellent.

Quality Not Quantity Counts

Simple messages from loved ones can mean a great deal. A few personally shared memories are all it takes to change a life.

Judy's Story

CASE STUDY

Judy came for intuitive counseling with me after her husband, Dave, committed suicide. She felt abandoned and alone. She had no idea how she could raise their three children without Dave. In fact, she struggled to get through every moment in the day.

Judy was unsure how she felt about life after death. She wanted to believe Dave had not disappeared forever, but she had nothing to prove otherwise.

While we were talking, I sent out a thought to the spirit world for help. I became aware of a man approaching me, and the love I felt from this man for Judy alerted me that it was her husband. Gently, I asked Judy if she would be open to me communicating with Dave. She indicated that she was willing to see what I came up with.

In my mind's eye, I saw her lying alone on a couch wrapped in an orange blanket. I heard Dave's voice say, "*Let her help you, Babe.*"

Dave also showed me that the roof of their home needed repairs. "*I would normally fix that myself,*" he said. Addressing his wife, he said, "*I'm so sorry I left you, Babe. I didn't know what else to do.*"

While more information could have followed, I didn't get a chance to find out. As soon as I mentioned the orange blanket, Judy reacted in shock.

"*That's Dave's blanket!*" she exclaimed. "*We each bought one, and mine is blue. I have been sleeping on the couch every night, rather than in our bed, wrapped up in his orange blanket. And Babe was his nickname for me - not Baby, just Babe.*"

Those small details made a huge difference to Judy. She confirmed the roof did need fixing and that Dave would have taken care of it in the past. She opened her mind to the possibility he was still watching over her. It gave her hope that he had not left her forever.

You can make a positive difference with just a few pieces of significant evidence from a loved one. If you feel drawn to mediumship, keep working on your gift.

The following extract from a mediumship reading puts together the features of high-quality evidence. The client, Zoe, recognizes the man in spirit as her father, and details are provided about his appearance, character and life. His heart-felt message is relevant and encouraging. This extract has been constructed to demonstrate the qualities of evidence and is not a factual account of a mediumship reading.

Extract from an Evidential Mediumship Message

Medium: *"Zoe, I have a man here who gives me the impression he is Dad or like a Dad to you. Can you relate to this?"*

(Zoe confirms her Dad has died).

Medium: *"I sense that he passed as an elderly man, somewhere in his 80s, and he loves you a great deal. He is grateful to you for helping him, especially towards the end, when he was very weak. Does this make sense?"*

(At this point, the evidence is still general. Zoe may have more than one older man in mind who she has helped. Some specific evidence is needed.)

Medium: *"He shows me that his hair was white and thinning in later years. I can smell smoke, so I know he was a smoker at some time. He worked with his hands, outside, and he gives me the impression of animals and farm machinery. This man loved the land. I sense an older style low-set house and vegetables in the backyard. The letter W feels significant to him, and I hear the nickname, Bill."*

Zoe: *"Yes, that's William, my Dad! He was known as Bill to just about everyone."*

Medium: *"Although your Dad dearly loved his home and family, he makes me feel he could also be a bit grumpy and short tempered. He wasn't much of a talker and liked to sit and read* his paper undisturbed, in his own chair. He shows me that late in life he was in and out of hospital, and that there are problems in the chest area. I can feel pressure on my chest, and I am short of breath. Can you confirm that?"

(Zoe confirms this is correct.)

Medium: "As I connect more closely with your Dad, he really wants to thank you for being there for him and for holding his hand in the hospital. He shows me that you sat with him on his right side and talked with him when he was in a coma. He wants you to know he did know you were there and says thank you."

(Pause for a while so the client can take this in. It's something that means a great deal.)

Medium: "Zoe, Dad says he knows life is tough for you, especially now you are on your own with the children, but 'hang in'. He is always watching over you. You are a strong woman and will get through it."

As a developing medium, you may only receive bits and pieces of a message or fragmented impressions. Know that this is natural. If you don't receive physical details, you may be able to build a strong sense of character and personal attributes that confirm the person's identity. If all you receive are vague impressions, begin with what you have. Jump in. The connection often builds as you go. Practice is the key.

If your client cannot recognize the spiritual communicator, thank the spirit and let them go. Focus on getting another link. It doesn't mean you are wrong, but it is pointless to continue.

Non-Evidential Spiritual Messages

Messages may also be received from spiritual guides and the client's soul. Messages from spiritual guides are often communicated to you by your guides; however, the client's guides will be contributing to the information shared.

Two examples follow.

Medium: "My spiritual guides make me aware that you have a strong desire to open a healing practice. They let me know that your guides are keen to support your work. Your guides encourage you to connect with them for at least fifteen minutes each day to strengthen the blending of energies between you."

Medium: "As I blend deeply with your energy, I sense that your soul chose to experience the lesson of service in this lifetime. That is why you have worked so hard helping others and why life has been tough. Don't give up. Your efforts are important, and your soul encourages you to hang in there. Look after yourself so you do not burn out."

The sources of these messages cannot be proven, and yet provided the messages are accurate and relevant to the client, they have worth.

The Nature of Evidence in Trance

While most well-known mediums work in an active, aware state, skillful trance mediums are the channel for spiritual intelligence, philosophy and creativity while working in a passive state.

Almost all contemporary trance mediums retain some level of awareness, although they do not know what is being spoken until the words leave their mouth. They may not hear their own voice except as a noise in the background, because they have trained their conscious mind to be subdued and passive while Spirit works through them.

The information received by a medium in trance is sometimes provided by a single spirit communicator, such as a doctor or healer in the spirit world. It may be one spirit who blends with the medium to talk with a loved one directly.

Information can also be provided by a team of spirits, with one spirit acting as the communicator for the group. This commonly occurs when the medium channels spiritual philosophy or teaching.

I received the following information about how trance teaching guides work with me.

> *"You ask if we have names. A river is made of water from several tributaries. They begin with individual names, yet merge so that the river is swift, strong and purposeful. It does not matter who we are as individuals. We offer you a channel of wisdom that combines the efforts of a group of Light Beings, and these beings will change as you evolve. Your commitment is the key to the channel's flow."*

Your spiritual helpers connect to you in trance through the energy of love. If a trance medium channels a frightening or negative message, they are projecting their subconscious fears or are linked to a spirit from a lower vibration.

Use your discernment in all situations involving trance. The quality of the communication or inspiration determines the value of the trance.

> *The energies of the spirits who blend with the medium should always enhance the medium's natural abilities or knowledge.*

If this fails to occur, then the medium is either linking with spirits from a lower level of consciousness or failing to hold the link in the first place.

> "To us, you are like shining jewels. We do not see you in the physical flesh but rather as vibrations of color and sound. We recognize you by the notes that you play.
> With every lesson learned, the jewels inside you shine more brightly. These are not gifts that can be grasped, for they must be earned. When you discover dew on a spider's web you see the beauty of every droplet, and yet if you were to try to catch that beauty with your hands, it would slip away. It is intangible.
>
> We see you as beings of potential who are already beautiful and whose lights already shine within. Protect your heart. Protect your song-lines. They are the essence of who you are."

Always set a clear intention and ask that your highest guides blend with you when you sit for trance. At every stage, you can emerge from trance or reject the spirits' influence. You don't 'go' anywhere. A passive mind does not mean that you have given up control of your wellbeing.

The following message which I received in trance holds a high and loving vibration. It exemplifies the cooperation and respect that our spiritual friends offer us and that we can offer them in return. That's the kind of energy I choose to work in.

"To us, you are like shining jewels. We do not see you in the physical flesh but rather as vibrations of color and sound. We recognize you by the notes that you play.

With every lesson learned, the jewels inside you shine more brightly. These are not gifts that can be grasped, for they must be earned. When you discover dew on a spider's web you see the beauty of every droplet, and yet if you were to try to catch that beauty with your hands, it would slip away. It is intangible.

We see you as beings of potential who are already beautiful and whose lights already shine within. Protect your heart. Protect your song-lines. They are the essence of who you are."

You can develop trance skills to inspire your writing, art, music, spiritual knowledge and any endeavor where your natural ability can be heightened. One of my favorite sayings is, '*Trance can only enhance.*'

Communicating Intuitive Evidence

While trance communication occurs without the medium's active involvement, most intuitive work occurs while the practitioner is working consciously with the client. How skillfully you, as an intuitive practitioner, share the evidence you receive, shapes the extent to which you provide encouragement and hope, or cause dismay and skepticism. Spiritual evidence, when communicated badly, can cause harm.

How would it feel to deliver your messages with confidence and competence, while at the same time building your client's confidence in you? The following chapter provides the next key to mastery, *Impeccable Communication*. This key provides you with the skills to become a skilled and confident channel for healing and hope.

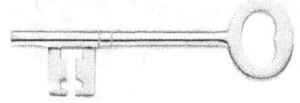

CHAPTER 5

IMPECCABLE COMMUNICATION

Key 5 Be The Channel For Healing And Hope

The word impeccable means 'in accordance with the highest standards.' Many years ago, I had the opportunity to witness what impeccable communication is not.

I was an audience member in a mediumship demonstration. There were approximately forty of us listening to the medium as she provided messages from the spirit world. Her work seemed to be on track because the recipients validated her information.

Then it happened.

The medium brought forward a father in the spirit world and connected him with a woman in the audience.

Without missing a beat, the medium said, *"Your father is laughing, because he can continue to abuse you now just like he did in the past, and you can't stop him. He says he hasn't changed a bit!"*

My heart leapt in my chest. I couldn't believe what I had heard. The woman collapsed in tears, but once the message was delivered, the medium moved on to someone else.

On so many levels, that message did harm.

- It terrified a woman without offering any help or support. How was she supposed to go home and deal with that?
- It publicly humiliated her.
- It broke all ethical principles about privacy.
- It showed no compassion.

The woman left soon afterwards, shepherded out by her friends.

That experience has remained with me for almost twenty years. It reminds me of the high level of responsibility and integrity needed by anyone who uses their intuitive gifts.

As a teacher, counselor, hypnotherapist and mentor, I have worked within ethical frameworks all my adult life. In spiritual work, strong ethics are essential, because clients place their trust in the practitioner and their messages.

The ethical framework I have developed is outlined below. You are welcome to use it and adapt it to your practice.

Ethical Principles

1. Maintain your client's right to privacy.

Ensure your client gives you permission to work intuitively. While it may seem obvious to *you* how you work, it may not be obvious to others. For example, a client who comes for an energy healing may not want their practitioner tuning into their marriage breakdown.

If you keep records, ensure you record only the information that is required, and that no-one else can access it. This might involve password protection on a computer or a locked filing cabinet. Record factual details only. Never record opinions, assumptions, judgments or emotional statements about your client.

If you offer intuitive readings, give any notes to your client or rip them up in their presence after your session.

2. Maintain your client's confidentiality.

Keep your client's identity and information confidential. If you discuss your work with another person, ensure you do not reveal the client's name or give away information that could identify them. Your client's trust in you is based on their belief you will honor their confidentiality.

3. Ensure every client knows you do not predict the future or give advice.

While some events in the future are set, you will not know what they are. Your client's outcomes may change if they alter their choices.

Never tell a client what to do or make legal, financial or medical predictions. Never promise what you cannot guarantee. If you do, you may be breaking consumer protection laws.

Even if a spirit communicator reveals something in your client's future, phrase it carefully so you do not take responsibility for the prediction.

4. Choose language carefully and accurately.

The word 'healing' is ambiguous. Make it clear that you do not promise recovery from any medical condition. Give each client a clear explanation of what 'healing' means in your practice so that your client has no misconceptions.

5. Uplift and resource your client. Help them explore possibilities to overcome challenges.

The client may not receive the information they hoped for, but your intuition can connect them with their strengths and options for moving forward. While you cannot change the client's life, you can help them widen their perspective. Do no harm. Never give information that would frighten or dismay.

A technique called the *feedback sandwich* frames a challenge in a positive way. It is a straightforward process of 3 statements:

1. A positive
2. The challenge
3. Another positive

Here is an example of a feedback sandwich:
1. You are a very strong person so,
2. even though you are under a lot of stress at work
3. you will be able to cope if you delegate some tasks and plan your time carefully.

6. Accurately describe the source of your intuitive insights.

Take responsibility for your evidence, and only refer to Spirit if you know the information comes from a spiritual source.

Rather than saying *"Spirit is telling me…"* or *"Spirit is showing me…"* if *you* are psychically feeling it, use phrases like "I sense," "I feel," or "I have the impression." Being honest in this way allows the client to understand where the information comes from.

Clients have a high level of faith in Spirit, so be careful what you attribute to the spirit world.

In order to build strong relationships with Spirit, you need to show integrity in this matter. Own what is your information and do not falsely quote Spirit.

7. Stay within your scope of competence.

Describe yourself honestly. Offer services in which you are competent.

Do not counsel unless you are qualified, and never tell a client what to do. Let them reach their own decisions as you help them explore options and possibilities.

8. Remain free from judgment and discrimination.

No matter what your client tells you, do not slander or criticize another person. Empathize with your client, but do not judge.

9. Match your message to your context.

Be mindful of your delivery style and choice of words, especially during a public demonstration. Sensitive information must be handled carefully, with an awareness of the client's wellbeing and privacy.

10. Remain emotionally composed.

You are the helper; you do not own the client's problems.

It does not help the client if the practitioner crumbles into tears and loses composure. Stay in your professional persona. Be empathetic while holding a safe, healing space for your client.

11. Refer to external support when required.

Always refer a client to external support services if you feel they need extra help. Have the names and numbers close by and encourage the client to make contact.

A Process for Communicating the Message

The following process allows you to explore and verify your evidence as you convey your message. This builds your confidence and also the client's confidence in you.

1. Start with one or more pieces of high-level information to elicit a 'Yes,' from the client.

2. Once you have a 'Yes,' drill down to draw out more details and specific information.

3. Seek feedback at regular intervals as you progress.

4. If you receive a 'No,' or 'I don't know,' return to the last piece of agreed information and work forward from that point.

The following scenarios demonstrate this process.

Scenario 1

In a mediumship reading, you sense a woman from the spirit world joining your client. You feel this spirit contact is an aunt on the client's mother's side of the family.

Start with high level information.

You say: *"I sense your aunt who joins us from the spirit world. She makes me feel she is a sister to your mother. Can you relate to that?"*

Had the client said, "No," you would widen the relationship to a paternal aunt or a friend of the mother who was *like an aunt* to the client.

In this case, the client says "Yes," so you begin to drill down to receive more details.

You say:

"Your aunt gives me the impression that she passed with an illness rather than a sudden event." (Pause for confirmation. The client says, "Yes.")

You continue:

"And this illness feels like cancer, because I see it spread from one place to another. Can you understand that?" (Opportunity for agreement or correction)

The client says, "Yes, it was cancer."

You say:

"That's right, and I also feel the breast is relevant. Would you know that?"

Let's assume the client said, "No," or "I don't know," to breast cancer.

You now return to the last agreed statement before moving on.

You say:

"*Okay, it wasn't breast cancer, but I am correct that your aunt had cancer?*" (Client nods) "*And it spread throughout her body?*" (Client says, "*That's right.*")

You say:

"*I am still feeling the chest area is involved. Was it lung cancer?*"

The client here may agree that the cancer was in the lungs or may still disagree. If you cannot gain any new, correct information, move on from the last point of agreement, which was that the aunt died from cancer.

When you re-state the agreed evidence, you keep the reading flowing and your energy stays higher than if you pause. It also allows time for new information to 'drop in' from Spirit, even though you are talking.

Once it is clear you have the connection to your client's aunt, blend your energy with the aunt as closely as you can, and continue the same process.

Gaining progressive feedback stops the client from silently disagreeing with you because you have made an error. If the client never had a maternal aunt, but the medium did not check, the rest of the information loses credibility.

Scenario 2

During a healing session you receive some impressions about your client. When the healing is over, the client invites you to share anything you sensed.

Your first statement begins at a high level.

You say:

"I sense a lot of stress around you at work. Does that make sense?" (The client agrees.)

Drill down into the feeling of this stress to gain more details.

You say:

"And you are having to take on more work than you can reasonably cope with, because your energy feels tired." (The client says, "I am very tired.")

You continue to sense more deeply into this situation.

"It's tough for you because I feel that you are very overloaded. It's like you just can't get a break."

(The client responds, "It's crazy at work. I can't get it out of my mind.")

Here is your chance to offer a safe and helpful option for the client to consider. You say:

"You know, I feel doing something fun would be really helpful for you right now. If you put aside some time to relax, it would give your mind a chance to wind down. Is there something you can think of?"

Your exploration allows you the opportunity to listen empathically as your client explores their feelings and options. By helping them widen their perspective, you also resource them to solve their own challenges.

When the Client Disagrees

Sometimes, you may be sure your information is accurate, but the client is unwilling to accept it. Do not take it to heart.

Never argue with a client or try to convince them to agree with you.

Re-interpret the evidence if you can and move on if necessary. Always be prepared to admit you may not be receiving the information accurately.

The exception is if a spirit person is talking with you directly. In that case, the client may understand the evidence later. Perhaps what the spirit communicator revealed is still to unfold.

Thank the client and invite them to remember what the spirit person said should new information come to light.

Handling Sensitive Information

It is often after a crisis or trauma that someone reaches out for help. Although you do not want to avoid distressing subjects, you can use gentle language to reduce the client's pain.

If you receive information from someone in spirit who lets you know they took their own life, you could use the following expressions:

"He lets me know he had a role in his passing."

"She is taking responsibility for crossing to the spirit world."

"He lets me know he felt there were no options left for him, and he just couldn't stay in this life any longer."

"I'm sensing a deep depression and a decision to escape this life. She just did not feel she could bear it any longer."

While statements like this may appear to hedge around the topic of suicide, they are less confronting than saying, *"I see he hanged himself by a rope in the garage."* You can always provide more details after opening with a gentle statement.

The spirit communicator already knows the distress their actions caused and will not want their loved ones to be further upset by images of their death.

Sometimes the spirit wants to apologize, explain their actions and encourage the client to live more positively. Always look for the most well-rounded message from any communicator who suicided, especially if they indicate they are now happier than before. Merely saying they took their life is no comfort.

Similarly, if someone has been murdered, or died as the result of someone else's carelessness, the following statements are helpful.

"She gives me the feeling that she was not responsible for her death. Her life was taken from her."

"He makes it clear that he did not choose to go when he did. He had a lot he was looking forward to. This was an accident that surprised him at the time. However, he has adjusted to his new life in the spirit world and is content now."

Use language that is natural to you, but it should be sensitive and empathetic when your client is struggling with trauma.

Likewise, if you sense your client has thoughts of self-harm, it is better to sound them out than ignore your instinct. A person who is still looking for help will likely tell you what they are planning. That allows you to seek help for them. For the person whose mind is made up, nothing you can offer, short of prayer and a miracle, is likely to make the difference.

The Difference Hope Makes

Meiling's Story

Meiling was feeling increasingly uneasy as the reading with her client, Wade, progressed.

The energy of despair seemed to surround him.

She opened the conversation as gently as she could.

"I'm sensing a huge weight around your heart," she ventured. *"It feels like you are really, really sad."*

Wade exhaled and nodded his head without comment. He did not meet her eyes.

Remaining connected with his energy, Meiling continued, *"I am so sorry you feel that way. I can sense such grief, like you have lost someone who was very special to you. You just don't know how to get over it. Does that make sense?"*

Meeting Meiling's eyes, Wade responded, "Yep. That about sums it up. I don't even know why I'm here. You can't change anything."

Meiling silently sent love and compassion to this man, lifting her energy towards the spirit world as she asked for guidance.

"I know I can't change anything in your life," she replied, "but I know you have a lot of strength. Even though you are in pain, I can sense that. You have had to overcome serious loss in the past, and you got through it. A relationship betrayal? Am I right?"

Again, Wade silently agreed, though his eyes looked more interested in Meiling's words than before.

"That's right," Meiling continued. "You had no idea how you would get through that, and yet you did."

She continued as gently as she could with what needed to be said.

"Wade, please be honest with me. Are you thinking about hurting yourself? Even taking your own life? Because when I connected with you, I got a strong impression you felt like there wasn't much worth staying around for."

Wade's eyes filled with tears as he hotly replied, "Well, since suicide was my big brother's way of coping, I thought I might give it a try. I don't know how to live without him. I don't even know who I am without him! We were best mates and he checked out of his life and left me here because it got hard. Well, it's hard for me too! So yeah, I'm thinking about it."

"I'm so sorry," Meiling said again, compassion filling her voice. "What was your brother's name?"

"Sam," said Wade, quietly.

"I can't even imagine how you are feeling and how much you must miss Sam," Meiling offered, "but I do know that your life still has purpose, even though it feels unbearably painful right now."

Using her psychic gifts, she continued, "Lots of people care about you. I see you surrounded by friends. You're a kind person. You listen to people. Actually, you are really good at fixing things too, cars especially. You have a talent for that."

"Yeah. I guess, but it doesn't help," Wade replied. "I don't enjoy anything anymore."

At that point, Meiling became aware of an energy joining her, a male person from the spirit world, and as she invited her guest closer, she knew it was her client's brother, Sam. The love she felt Sam emanating for his younger brother was overwhelming.

"Actually, your brother is here now," Meiling said. "He really wants to communicate something to you. Are you willing to hear it?"

"I guess so," Wade stammered. "Really? Yes. Definitely!"

Maintaining her composure, Meiling encouraged Sam to blend his thoughts and feelings with her energy, aware of the excitement Sam felt to finally be able to talk to his brother.

She continued the reading, bringing forward special memories the brothers had shared. She described Sam's wicked sense of humor, his love of endurance motor-bike riding, and passed on his message that he had been severely depressed when he took his own life. He had thought there were no options, but now he sees that there was plenty to live for, if he had only asked for help. Sam sought Wade's forgiveness and asked that his younger brother live his life to the full. Sam promised Wade that he would always watch out for him from the spirit world and share Wade's adventures.

By the time Sam's energy withdrew, Meiling's client looked brighter than when he had arrived. Although there had been many tears, Wade felt less sad and hopeless than before.

Before Wade left, Meiling had two questions for him.

"Can you promise me that you are no longer considering harming yourself?" she asked. "That you have changed your mind about that?"

"I promise." Wade answered. "Not after that. Not now I know that Sam's okay and is still part of my life."

"Great, and will you take the number for a counseling service?" Meiling added, passing a card towards him. "There is one in our area who works with all kinds of tough issues. Would you consider calling them? I'm not a counselor. I think you would benefit from the right support."

"Okay," Wade responded, accepting the card. "I will call them. Thanks. When can I come back and hear from Sam again?"

"I would be very happy to read for you again, Wade, but leave it for several months. It is important that you work through how you are feeling first. Give me a call in about 5 months, unless there is an emergency and you really need to see me."

With that, the reading wound up, and Wade left, a less despairing man than before.

Meiling showed impeccable communication in delivering her message. Her compassion and care for her client gave him the strength to continue his life.

You now have five keys, each of which unlocks an important door to excellence in using your intuitive gifts. However, your reputation as a polished professional relies on more than using your intuitive skills. Your clients want a quality experience from the moment they contact you until the session has concluded, and even beyond. When you ensure every aspect of your service is at a high standard, your client feels comfortable. For that, you need a quality checklist to guide you. My gift to you in the following chapter is a quality checklist to ensure you have a structure for a good session, every time.

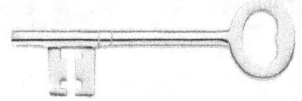

CHAPTER 6

THE STRUCTURE OF A GOOD SESSION

Key 6 A Quality Checklist for a Professional Process

Your intuitive skills create strong foundations for your work; however, like building a home, it's how everything comes together that counts. The structure needs to be sound or the home will be unstable. Your process for working with your gifts also needs to be sound. You need to appear competent and professional, from the booking to the conclusion.

Before you accept any bookings, be clear about your practice.

- What services do you offer?
- How will you deliver them?
- How much will you charge
- How can the client pay you?

Open your mind to wider possibilities than you first imagined. Can you offer some services using technology such as Skype, Messenger, email or phone? Know your options before you promote yourself or book clients.

Your Quality Checklist

Your Recorded Phone Message

When you cannot answer the phone, clients need a recorded message that invites them to leave their details.

Practice the message until you sound professional and confident. Include your name, business name, and ask the prospective client to leave their first name, message and phone number after the tone. Promise to call them as soon as possible.

Here is one example of a phone message.

"Thank you for calling Michelle at The Academy of Spiritual Practice. I'm sorry I am unable to speak with you at the moment; however please leave your first name, a brief message and your phone number, and I will contact you as soon as possible. I look forward to talking with you soon. Have a great day."

The Phone Call to Book

Be organized. Have your appointment schedule in front of you.

Be courteous, positive and engaged. Allow at least ten minutes for the call. However, do not let the client tell you more than is needed because then you cannot later claim that information as evidence.

Elicit what the client seeks. Is it within your skillset? You want positive feedback and happy clients. Never be afraid to refer a client to someone else if you cannot deliver what they want. If someone wants to talk with their Mum in spirit, and you find mediumship challenging, refer them to another practitioner.

Assure the potential client that every aspect of their session is confidential.

Describe your services and how you work. Are you a psychic? A medium? A psychic medium? A spiritual healer?

Explain your background, relevant training, level of experience and why you do what you do.

The importance of this was highlighted one day when one of my clients complained bitterly to me about a therapist he had just seen. At the end of the session with this therapist, he had refused to pay.

"*All the therapist did,*" said the client, "*was get me to hold my arm out straight while he pressed down on it over and over again. What kind of rubbish was that?*"

Clearly, this client had consulted a kinesiologist without understanding what kinesiology involved. Fortunately, he paid me without complaint, because he knew what I offered and how I worked.

In a healing service:

Explain that the word 'healing' does not imply recovery from a condition. You work energetically and intuitively. You do not offer promises, health advice or predictions. An improvement of wellbeing can occur on levels that are not visible, such as less stress, calmer emotions, balanced chakras and so on.

If touch is involved, let the client know what to expect and gain their permission.

In a psychic reading:

Explain that the only promise you make is that you will do your best. You do not offer predictions, legal, medical or financial advice. The future changes with the client's actions. You will help them see options and possibilities with your intuitive gifts.

In a mediumship reading:

The only promise you make is that you will do your best. Explain that you cannot guarantee that the person they wish to contact will come through. You cannot control who will be present.

Fees and service

Explain the cost of your session or service and payment options. Outline cancellation and refund policies if relevant.

If you both feel comfortable, take the client's first name, their phone number and book them in.

Provide them with your address, their appointment day and time. Tell them you will remind them with a text on the morning of their appointment.

Check for any questions. End the call in a friendly manner.

The Enquiry Phone Call

CASE STUDY

Brett phones John from *Intuitance Healing* to book an appointment.

John answers the phone: *"Yep. John here. Who's this?"*

> Brett: "Oh. Hi. My name's Brett, I'm interested in booking a session with you for energy balancing. I haven't had one before."
>
> John: "Ok. How's Tuesday, 3 pm? The cost is $80 for the hour. $115 for 90 minutes."
>
> Brett: "Um, can you just tell me a bit about how you work, please?"
>
> John: "Yep. What do you want to know? It's pretty straightforward. What don't you understand? It's energy balancing. You'll enjoy it. It'll be good for you."
>
> Brett: "I think I'll leave it for a while and get back to you. Thanks, anyway. Bye."

Let's re-wind that call and start again.

> Brett phones John to book an appointment.
>
> John answers the phone: "Hi, this is John from Intuitance Healing. How can I help?"
>
> Brett: "Hi. I'm interested in booking a session with you for energy balancing. I haven't had one before."
>
> John: "Ok. No problem. So, you haven't had an energy balance before? Let me tell you about it and how I work."
>
> Brett: "Ok, cool. I was wondering about that."

> John: "I've been doing energy balances for about eight years now and I work intuitively. I connect to the energies of the universe and ask the guides who work with me to help me. I will tune into your aura and your energy centers, they're called chakras, and help balance the flow of energy throughout your system. I work above your body in your energy field. How does that sound? Is there more you would you like to know?"
>
> Brett: "That sounds good to me. Can you help me with my back problem?"
>
> John: "Energy balancing supports all healing, but I can't promise to cure a medical issue. You need to work with your doctors on that. A balanced energy system does promote your general wellbeing though. It helps on several levels."
>
> Brett: "That's ok. I understand. Can I book?"
>
> John: "Sure. Let me tell you about costs and options, and we can work out what best suits. I have EFTPOS by the way, so payment is easy."

The conversation continues, and Brett feels much more confident than in the first scenario.

Before the Session

Prepare your environment. Make sure any tools and materials are organized. Remember tissues.

If using scent to clear the room, do so well in advance of the client's arrival. Some clients' sinuses react to incense and essential oils. Asthma may also be triggered by smell.

Avoid specific religious icons as they may not reflect your client's beliefs.

Consider your personal safety. Even if you are alone, create the impression that someone is close by, and never let the client sit between you and your safe exit.

Think hard before working with a stranger if you are alone. Always have a backup plan, a phone or someone who knows what's happening.

Step into your professional persona and affirm you are ready to work. *"Here I am! I'm ready to work."*

Meditate to calm your mind and emotions. Sit in the Power, listen to music and use the strategies that build and sustain your energy.

Set a clear intention to be of service for the client's highest good.

Let your spiritual guides know you are ready to work and thank them for their assistance.

The Session

Consider the client's comfort. Offer that they might use the bathroom and have a glass of water ready for them when they arrive.

Establish rapport. Be friendly, confident and professional.

Ask the client if they have had a similar session, service or reading, how long ago and how they found it. Limit this conversation to a few minutes. If something went very well, you may be able to build on that. If something occurred that they did not like, it is helpful to know.

Ask the client what they hope to experience. You want to discover their greatest need or reason for contacting you.

Honor the client. Connect to them with compassion.

Take charge. Monitor the time and lead the process.

For a Healing

If you are collecting information about your client, complete an intake form and a disclaimer form.

There are many examples of client intake and disclaimer forms on the internet. Find one that reflects your requirements and adapt it to suit your practice. Whether you complete records or do a verbal intake, gather only the details that relate to the client's booking. Too much information may interfere with your intuition and invade the client's privacy. Stick to what you need to know.

If you plan to share your intuitive impressions, let the client know when that will occur.

Begin your process. Ask to be a clear, true channel for the healing energies of the Source and maintain your connection.

Share any information sensitively and ethically.

For A Reading

Limit what the client tells you about themselves.

Explain that they can help by having an open attitude, but you do not want them to feed you information. You will ask for feedback to check you are 'on track' and sometimes you may need to interpret evidence differently.

Elicit their reason for coming. What is their need?

Maintain your professional composure throughout.

A Psychic Reading

- Connect with the client. Send them compassion, hold a personal item or offer some healing.
- Begin with the client's priority. Focus on the reason the client has provided for wanting to see you.
- General topics include family, career, relationships, travel, hobbies, personal wellbeing, study, finances.
- Start with high level information to gain agreement and then dig deeper into details. Seek regular feedback.
- Use tools if you choose.
- Resource and uplift the client. Do no harm.
- Alert the client 5 minutes before the reading closes.
- Check for any final questions.

A Mediumship Reading

- Lift your energy and invite one spirit communicator at a time who is known and recognized by the client to join you. Open your mind to all relationships so the best communicator steps forward. (Remember that animals in spirit may also communicate.)
- Blend your energy with the spirit communicator's energy so that the connection is close.
- Allow the spirit communicator to lead the message. The message may come in a blend of your senses - sight, sound, smell, feeling, taste and knowing.
- Provide the best evidence you can. Aim for a blend of facts, shared memories, personality traits and a personal message.

- Establish the spirit communicator's reason for coming. What do they want the client to know?
- Alert the client 5 minutes before the reading will close.
- Check for any final questions.

Tips if the Client Appears to be Blocking You

Some clients arrive with an attitude that is less open and more skeptical than you might prefer. Remind them that the more relaxed they are, the easier it is for you to make strong connections. It's not a test. You are here to help.

Remember that a client who appears obstructive may just be self-protective of delicate issues in their life. Don't judge them. Remark on their attitude and explore it. Are they testing you or are they anxious? Commenting on what you notice is often enough to dissolve any blocks.

Ask them to take some deep breaths and reassure them that you have their wellbeing foremost in your mind.

Keep your power up throughout. If you lose the link, re-focus and lift your auric energy. Think positive thoughts and re-cap on the agreed evidence.

If a client becomes rude, abusive or threatening, ask them to leave immediately and give a full refund. Your safety comes first.

Closing the Session or Reading

- Check the client is satisfied.
- Offer any referrals you feel may be needed.
- Accept payment and offer a receipt.
- Thank the client and ask for a testimonial if the reading or service went well.
- Offer your business card and invite the client to refer potential clients to you.

After the Session or Reading

Clear the energies in your space. Smudge, flush the room with light, say a cleansing prayer or use your own process as you intend that the energy in the room is transformed.

Imagine yourself under a shower of light and release all energies and feelings the session or reading raised within you.

> *You are only the channel or messenger. Let it all go.*

Remember to thank your spiritual team and ground yourself. You might also choose to eat or drink something, walk outside or have a shower.

Releasing the energy of your session or service allows you to replenish your energies after working. However, it is not just after working that you need to care for yourself.

Intuitive work requires you to be strong physically, emotionally, mentally and spiritually. The quality of your intuition suffers when you do not have the health and balance to hold the vibration needed for your work. Prioritizing your self-care is an essential key in your intuitive toolkit. Wisdom in self-care helps you to sustain connections and assist your clients in a way that equally rewards them and you. The following chapter addresses the seventh key - looking after you too.

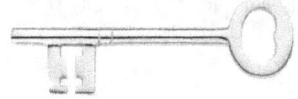

CHAPTER 7

LOOKING AFTER YOU TOO

Key 7 Wisdom in Self-Care

My Dad had a silver alto saxophone that he cherished. I remember the brown wooden case it was stored in and the indigo velvet lining that cradled the instrument when it was put away. I remember the soft cloth my Dad kept inside the case to wipe the thin wooden reed in the mouth-piece and the fact he never handled the saxophone carelessly or roughly. The instrument was in the same good condition when he passed away at ninety-six, as it was when he was forty, and my son still plays it today.

Dad understood that if he didn't look after his instrument, neither he nor his saxophone would perform at a professional standard.

As the instrument of your gift, you deserve to be treated with respect. The standard of your intuitive work relies on your wellbeing.

If you have ever heard a guitar or other stringed instrument when it is out of tune, you know that it doesn't matter how well the player knows the music or moves their fingers, the sound is disappointing.

This analogy applies to your self-care. When you look after your physical, emotional, mental and spiritual health, you offer your gifts and your spiritual team the best chance of a successful experience. However, if you neglect your energy levels and are rundown, lethargic or unwell, your instrument will be out of tune and your gifts will struggle to work.

Rather than tuning strings, as you would an instrument, you need to attune to the vibration that aligns you with vitality, your gifts and your soul's purpose. It takes only a few minutes to achieve this.

Vibrational Attunement

- Sit or stand; either is fine so long as your back is straight. Lift your focus and energy towards the Source and ask to be attuned so that your vibration aligns with your life's lessons and soul's purpose. If there is something you need to achieve in the next few weeks, ask that you are aligned for the highest outcome.
- Next, release that thought and relax. You may feel subtle energies moving around you, or you may not feel anything new. The attunement takes fewer than five minutes. Metaphorically, a vibrational attunement realigns your inner compass to your true North.

Respect Your Body's Signals.

Prior to working with my intuitive gifts, I was a teacher, adding roles like Disability Support Coordinator, Student Support Officer and College Counselor to my main function. I was frequently tired, given I also had two children living at home.

Like many busy people, I did not consider the impact of my workload on my health. I slept poorly, but nothing slowed me down. I completed extra qualifications, applied for new support roles, and finally the crunch came.

I developed chronic fatigue and it took me almost two years to recover. During that time, meditation and connecting with my spiritual guides helped me enormously and one day I heard the following words from a loving guide.

"A desert cannot replenish itself. Only an oasis, fed by an underground spring, provides sustenance and renewal to the weary traveler. Become an oasis by nurturing yourself. Control the flow of your energy so that as you empty in one direction, you are filled from another. You will then have the reserves to continue your journey."

> "A desert cannot replenish itself. Only an oasis, fed by an underground spring, provides sustenance and renewal to the weary traveler. Become an oasis by nurturing yourself. Control the flow of your energy so that as you empty in one direction, you are filled from another. You will then have the reserves to continue your journey."

I realized that although I had been caring for everyone else, I had not honored myself. I believed the wellbeing of others mattered above my own. The importance of respecting myself is a lesson I have remembered.

Stay aware of how you feel and respond to any signals of discomfort. Your work may be your passion, but holistic health allows you to sustain it.

Signs of Stress and Burnout

Burnout happens when a person ignores the signs of stress. Rather than feeling tired or down for a few days, which happens with stress, a person experiencing burnout is tired almost all the time and finds it hard to cope, every day. If you feel lethargic, perpetually tired, anxious or depressed, seek help. Talk with your doctor, a counselor or a trusted friend.

Connect with other professionals who can support you or a professional association in your field. Debrief and let yourself be cared for, rather than being the helper.

Make sure you have downtime to enjoy life, and be vigilant about releasing all the problems your clients shared with you. In the shower, imagine any heavy energies washing away as a stream of light renews you.

Connect with your Inner Spirit

Any activity that makes you feel alive and connected to your spirit is a personal spiritual practice. Your spiritual practice should be enjoyable, and not something that feels like work. Walking in nature may be what you love. Swimming in the ocean cleanses your aura. Chanting is excellent for calming and lifting your vibration. Yoga aligns and strengthens you physically, mentally, emotionally and spiritually. It doesn't matter what you choose as long as it energizes you and connects you back to you.

As well as active strategies, listen to the messages of your soul and your spiritual team. Sit in the Power, lift your energy and invite your guides to blend their mind and energy with yours. Fifteen minutes a day in communion with your soul and with your spiritual guides deepens your holistic health and spiritual gifts.

Quieten your mind and withdraw from the outside world. What would your soul like you to know? Are you being kind to yourself?

In the same way that you offer compassion to others, let compassion flow through you, for you. You can choose that.

Live a Healthy, Grounded Life

Practice practical spirituality. You are on Earth because your soul chose to experience life. Do not try to escape it.

Finding a balance between the Earthly and spiritual planes is important, as the following case study illustrates.

Natalia's Story

CASE STUDY

Natalia's dedication to her spirituality was beyond question. She woke at 5.30 each morning so she had an hour to quietly communicate with her soul and guides before she got out of bed.

She was a healer who knew her intention to be of service really mattered. She devoted her non-work time to spiritual development courses, reading spiritual books, following spiritual leaders on YouTube and discussing healing with everyone around her. You may know someone who reminds you of Natalia.

I met Natalia when she began experiencing disconcerting symptoms. She felt as though she was not quite in her body, but instead was floating slightly above or beside herself. This created disorientation, anxiety and balance problems.

The effects were amplified after long periods of sitting in high spiritual energy, something Natalia thought was essential to her progress.

Because Natalia had not been balancing herself with grounded energy, she was dissociating from her body and the world.

I explained to Natalia that while it is natural to be passionate about our spiritual path, we must also remain grounded.

> *We are spirits who incarnated as human beings to anchor spiritual lessons in a practical environment. If we ignore our humanness, we block the experiences we need.*

I encouraged Natalia to immerse herself in a wider range of interests.

- Living near a beach, she walked each day on the sand and enjoyed the energy of the ocean.
- In the past, she had grown her own herbs and salad vegetables, and so she revived this hobby, connecting her hands with the soil.
- In her spare time, she chatted with friends about their interests and read books for enjoyment, not just to further her spiritual knowledge.

A grounded and balanced approach was what Natalia needed to stay present in her physical body. Within a few weeks her unpleasant symptoms had resolved.

Practice Healthy Habits

Our habits play a large role in our self-care. Evaluate your habits and make any changes that would improve your wellbeing. Remember the importance of sleep, time to relax, fun, good nutrition, movement, positive thinking and positive relationships.

Healthy habits help sustain a strong, vital auric field, which is essential for our energy management.

Set Healthy Boundaries in Work and Life

One of the main causes of stress for practitioners who work in the helping professions, is the inability to say, *"No, I am sorry. I cannot do that right now."*

It is easy to believe that unless we are available for every person who needs us, we are not giving enough. This is not true. You are responsible for your wellbeing. Like every other person's life, your life matters.

> *What does it suggest about how you value yourself if you always put yourself last?*

Be clear about how you will work and when. Do not accept behavior that diminishes you or reduces your self-confidence. Establish healthy boundaries and do not take on the responsibilities or burdens of clients or other adults. Their life is their responsibility. Your life is yours.

Ongoing Professional Development

Continue to take opportunities for skill and knowledge development. Your gifts evolve in the same way that other skills improve with practice. With higher levels of understanding and competence, your confidence soars. Networking through professional development is also very helpful for discovering creative synergies with other practitioners.

Your commitment to strategies that promote your self-care is vital to your physical, emotional, mental and spiritual health.

In a similar way, you need to implement carefully planned strategies when you set up and market your business. A successful business seldom evolves by chance. Research and planning create a solid basis on which to build your professional intuitive practice.

The following chapter provides simple guidelines for setting up and marketing your intuitive practice. Becoming business-wise is another vital key to longevity and success as you put your spiritual gifts to work.

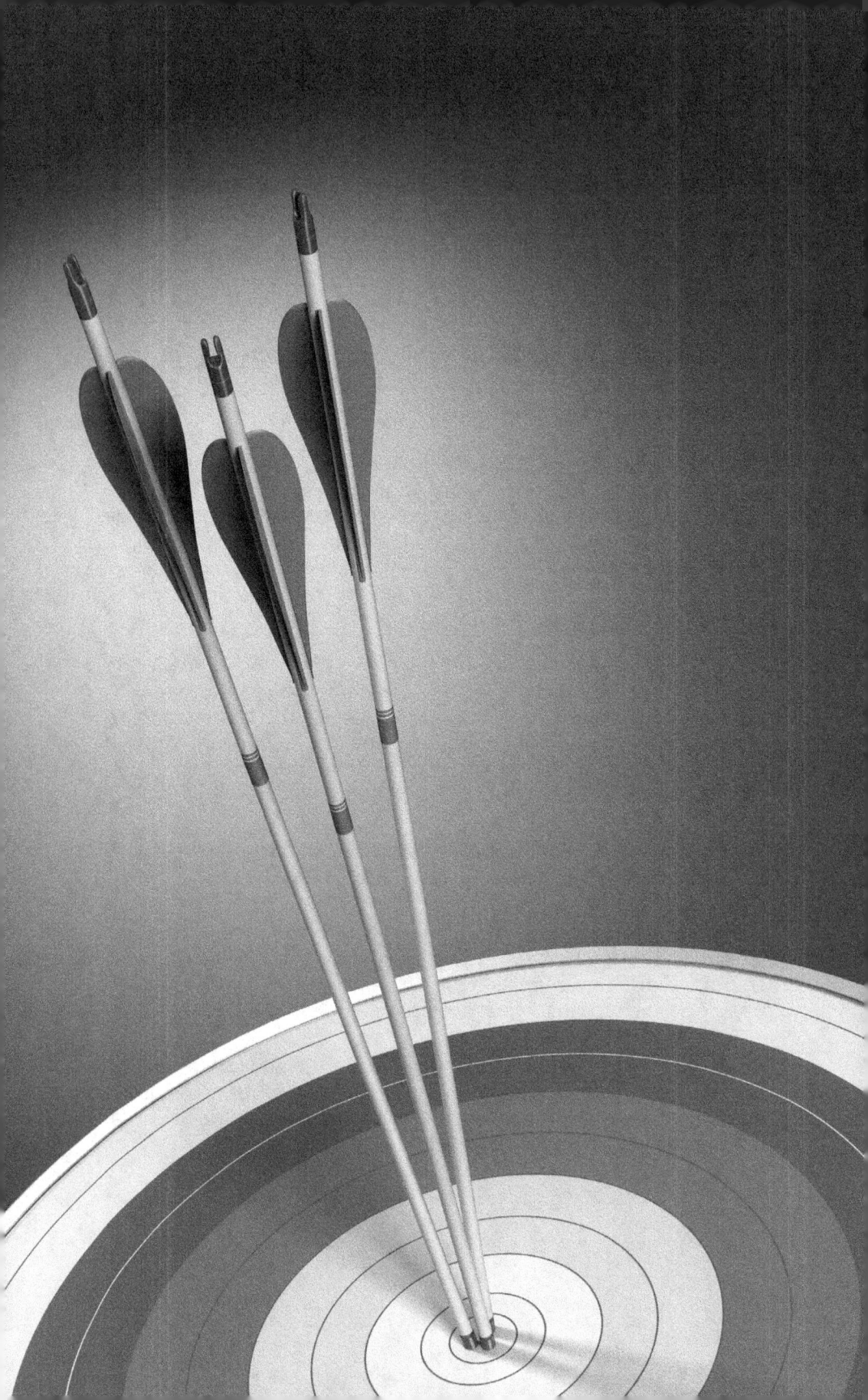

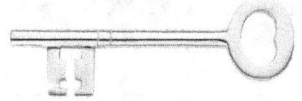

CHAPTER 8

SET UP AND MARKET YOUR PRACTICE

Key 8 Become Business-Wise

Passion is a great motivator, yet you need more than passion when establishing a business. You also need business-sense.

Like any important decision, the benefits and costs of change need to be weighed carefully within the framework of your life. Although you might yearn to 'jump ship' and change jobs immediately, lessons sometimes occur in situations where you feel least comfortable. The timing to make a switch from one career to another has to be right.

> **Spiritual and Physical Law**
> **CASE STUDY**
> Ellen believed in the Law of Attraction and focused on the rightful abundance she knew was waiting for her when she opened her spiritual practice. Morning and evening, she visualized success, imagining the clients who would be helped by her intuitive skills. She sent her positive intentions out to the universe and one day, without warning, she quit her job and rented a shop in the main street of her town.

> It was a bit impulsive, Ellen knew, but she was sure the universe would not let her down.
>
> Unfortunately, clients did not stream to her practice the way she had imagined, and the rent on her shop, combined with other expenses, was more than Ellen was earning. She was dismayed and felt let down by her guides when two months later, she had to relocate to her own home.
>
> Ellen had not been abandoned by her spiritual guides. She had forgotten that she lived in a physical world. Although her visualization and positive thinking were important, they were only half of what had to be done. She had not taken the practical steps that were needed to manifest her plans on the Earth plane. Energetically, she had everything aligned for success, but in a practical sense, there was a big hole where research and planning should have been.

Ellen's story is not unfamiliar to me. I know of several businesses that have folded because passion was not supported by business-sense.

I maintained my mainstream job for four years while I slowly built my intuitive practice. I saw clients after working hours and on weekends but did not lose financial stability. Taking my time allowed me to understand what setting up a practice entailed, and I did it without urgency. I did it without the stress of financial instability, which could have lowered my vibration and interfered with my spiritual gifts.

Think Outside the Box

It is very exciting to consider opening a professional practice. Open your mind to as many possibilities as you can. The best way forward may be something you have not thought of yet.

Creatively consider the services you offer. Can you add an online or technology-based aspect to reach a wider client base?

In my clinic, I offered intuitive counseling and hypnotherapy, spiritual healing, and intuitive readings. My readings were also offered via phone, Facebook Messenger, Viber, Skype, typed email or digital recording. I looked for opportunities to reach clients where and how they preferred. I recorded meditation and hypnosis audios which were offered to clients and sold online.

In my regional district, I still teach spiritual development workshops, both individually and in partnership with a colleague. We operate this partnership through a Facebook business page and find Facebook a great way to reach interested participants.

I mentor students in spiritual development both online and face to face, guiding them to connect to their intuitive gifts. Most importantly, I help people awaken to the realization that life on Earth is a small part of a much longer journey. Once this life ends, they will return to their home in the spirit world, where loving friends await them.

Every life, through the lessons the soul chose before its human birth, has purpose and meaning.

Open your creative mind to the possibilities that extend beyond the obvious options you have thought of in the past. You can begin to build your business slowly over time.

Marco's Tips

Psychic medium, Marco Della Valle, took the leap of faith to leave his job in marketing and transition to a full-time psychic medium. Prior to his decision, Marco had offered after-work readings in the evening and on weekends. He steadily built a client-base, and finally the long waiting period for prospective clients to get an appointment gave Marco the courage to switch careers.

Marco had taken the time to establish his practice, build his reputation and hone his gifts before he changed careers permanently. His business continues to thrive today.

I asked Marco to share what he had learned in establishing his own intuitive practice. He provided me with the following thoughts.

- "Be active on Social Media.
- Start doing consultations part-time to build a clientele before going full-time.
- Don't be afraid to set up a home-practice.
- Decide how often you want to work and stick to your hours.
- Have a system and don't allow yourself to be contacted at all hours of the night. Clients will get used to your availability and you don't want to burn out before you even go full-time.
- Treat your intuitive work as a business. It's your time, energy and income. Although it's spiritual and about helping people, make sure you run it in the background like any other small business owner.
- Plan how much money you need to make each week, before you decide to leave your traditional paid work.
- Plan the work and then work your plan to make sure you keep yourself afloat.
- Don't let fear stop you. You are not there to be judged; you are there to be of service."

Marco's suggestions show a practical and sensible approach to establishing a practice. Remember, there is a difference in mindset that is required when you change from being an employee, with a regular pay check, to becoming an independent entrepreneur and a small business owner of an intuitive practice. It is a new identity that you need to step into, a new way of thinking that your brain needs to learn. Stepping into that business the way that Marco suggests, and the way that I did it too, means your business grows as you grow.

> *By the time you're ready to step into the role of a full-time small business owner of an intuitive practice, every physical cell in your body and every neural connection is aligned and confident with your new vision.*

You've done the ground work. You've honed your craft and become business savvy. Your spiritual guides and supporters know how to help you create exactly what you want for your business and your clients now. You and the universe are aligned.

Business-Sense is Common-Sense

A good mix of common-sense and thorough business research are important ingredients when you are establishing a business. There is no need to feel overwhelmed and make hasty decisions.

Your first question is, *"Do my plans match the definition of operating a business in my country and even the state or province that I live in?"*

The answer to this question will vary depending on the guidelines applicable to where you reside or intend setting up business. Guidelines will exist that determine if your activities are considered recreational or constitute a business.

In many countries, you are engaged in a business if you conduct commercial or professional activities to produce goods and services for profit.

Research whether your planned activities constitute a business where you live and what that means in the setup-stage of your business.

If you are ready to establish a business, the following steps provide you with a starting point for further investigations.

Prior to Starting the Business

- **Choose your Business Structure.**

    In Australia for example, you may choose to establish yourself as a sole proprietor (sole trader) if you are the only person operating your business. This means that you are responsible for the business' decisions and liabilities. You will pay personal tax on the profits you have earned and, if you choose, you may be able to work under your own name. This is a straightforward way to set up a business and many single owner businesses begin this way. However, as a sole proprietor, you are not protected from debts your business may incur.

    A limited liability company is often chosen as the preferred business structure, especially as the business expands. A limited liability company gives you some protection from liability for the business' debts. What this means is that your personal assets such as your personal bank account, car, and home will have protection if your business incurs debts, unlike if you operated as a sole proprietor.

    In the United States for example, a limited liability company is called an LLC. An LLC helps protect your personal assets from business debts and lawsuits.

    Every country will have their own regulations and structures. Do your research to ensure you comply with all requirements. Consult a financial expert and the relevant government websites for the regulations and requirements that apply to you. A search on your internet browser will take you to the appropriate government websites if you include 'set up a business' and your area of residence.

- **Choose and Register Your Business Name.**

Unless you are a sole proprietor, it is likely you need to work under a business name for tax purposes. Before you invest in any marketing materials, research whether your preferred business name is available. Again, an internet search in your state or country will reveal the organization you need to approach to claim and register your business name. There may be an annual fee. (Once you establish if the business name is available to register, it is also worth establishing whether the domain name is available to purchase.)

- **Assess Potential Expenses.**

Investigate the expenses you will incur in your business setup and then the ongoing expenses like power, insurances, website development and hosting, promotional materials, professional tools, clothing, professional memberships and furniture.

- **Consider Where You Will Base Your Practice.**

Will you work from home or will you rent a space? What best fits into your budget planning?

If you intend to rent a space to work, look for the venue that best supports you as you build your clientele. Some venues charge rent based only on what you earn, while others set a daily or weekly rent payment. Paying the same amount of rent each week regardless of the number of clients you see rapidly eats into your income and viability if you have a quiet week.

Before signing a rental property agreement, make sure you will have the income to justify the expense, or seek a space that offers flexibility. With research you can find venues that allow you to pay only for the hours you need.

If you do decide to rent a venue, you could investigate whether another practitioner could share or rent the space when you are not using it, to offset your expenses.

Working from home may be your solution if you have a private and professional space available. You will not appear professional if your space is cluttered, noisy or prone to interruptions from phones, children or pets.

Working from home gives you the flexibility to work anytime you choose. It also saves the time lost and the cost incurred by travel.

Check relevant government regulations about running a business from your home. There may be parking, signage, building access and other regulations that you must follow. Ensure that local and state regulations allow you to work from your home and you understand how to do so legally.

If you are working from home, consider your safety and privacy. You might consider a door- buzzer that sounds in another part of the house should you get into trouble. Never create the impression you are alone. Have strategies in place for your safety and the privacy of your clients.

- **Consider your brand.**

If you have not yet decided on your brand, send your ideas out to friends and clients and ask for feedback. What colors, logo and style will represent you?

Setting Up Your Business

- **Seek Financial Advice.**

Gaining professional advice from an accountant or business lawyer saves worry and error. They will explain the tax and financial implications of your business.

Will you lose any government payments if you add a new income stream? Will your tax bracket change?

How much income do you need to earn before you are considered a business? How much income do you need to have earned before you claim your business expenses?

Do not assume that everything you spend on setting up your business can be claimed immediately.

- **Set Up a Business Bank Account.**

Establish a business account so that your finances can be tracked separately from personal finances.

- **Take Steps to Comply with Tax Requirements.**

This may mean applying for a tax file number if you do not already have one.

- **Take Out Insurance.**

Whether you have a thriving practice or see only a few clients a week, insurance is a necessity. As well as Third Party Liability Insurance, I suggest you also gain Professional Indemnity Insurance. Professional Indemnity Insurance offers you with protection should claims be made against the quality of your services.

Gaining insurance for practitioners who work in complementary fields is not always easy.

I found that once I joined a professional organization and had my modalities accredited, I was eligible for insurance. The International Institute for Complementary Therapists (IICT) recognizes modalities such as psychic work, mediumship and spiritual healing. Once they approve your competence in the skills you apply for, you can apply for third party and professional indemnity insurance from their affiliated insurer. IICT is only one example of how to obtain insurance cover for your business. Please research the right association and insurer for you.

- **Keep Accurate and Relevant Business Records.**

Whether you use computer software, spreadsheets or other tools, always maintain accurate, comprehensive records of your business income and expenses from the outset. Check the reports you will need to provide for tax or other agencies in your country and make sure you have captured this information.

- **Research Successful Competitors.**

What can you learn about their practice and business methods? Research the cost of their services and consider where you will place yourself in relation to their fees.

Do not be tempted to be the cheapest practitioner. Many customers equate the price of a service with the quality it implies.

- **Purchase a Domain Name if You Intend to Have a Website.**

Research guidelines around effective domain names before you purchase. Design and purchase business cards that align with your brand and sell your message.

- **Comply with Relevant Legislation.**

Ensure you understand the requirements of legislation in your state or country. Consider legislation for:

Consumer protection. This is very important. Make no claims you cannot fulfill.

Anti-discrimination

Privacy. Know your obligations about collecting, retaining and storing personal information.

Disability, including access requirements for people with disabilities

Workplace health and safety

Specific industry legislation

When I began my intuitive business I worked from home, registered a business name, gained insurance through a professional organization, opened a business bank account, printed business cards, created a Facebook business page, and began working. These basic steps were all I needed to get started.

> When I began my intuitive business I worked from home, registered a business name, gained insurance through a professional organization, opened a business bank account, printed business cards, created a Facebook business page, and began working. These basic steps were all I needed to get started.

You can build your business as you grow. Later you can add extras like a website or other social media pages.

Business Promotion and Marketing

Define your marketing strategy. This will include decisions about your price, what you offer (including whether you have packaged your sessions), how you deliver your services and how you promote them.

Here are some strategies to help you promote yourself and your work.

Over-Deliver.

Word of mouth and client recommendations attract new clients without extra expense.

> *If your clients become your 'fans' they will talk about their experience with you, and if they are disappointed, they will talk about it even louder.*

When you over-deliver, you pack your service full of perceived value. The client receives more than they expected, which in turn makes them feel heard, validated and nurtured.

Consider adding a little extra time to what you advertise, such as an extra five or ten minutes to show you are not watching the clock.

You may be able to add another skill to the session. Keep it simple. A 3 card oracle card reading after a healing? Five minutes of healing after a reading? A follow-up email to see how they feel after your service? A discount for a second session or a new client booking through their referral?

Re-Package Your Service.

Look for opportunities to package your gifts and promote new skills. Could you now offer intuitive insights that you were hesitant about before? Would you feel comfortable adding intuition to mainstream work, promoting services such as intuitive massage, intuitive counseling, intuitive aromatherapy, intuitive kinesiology?

Consider Free Bonuses.

Could you record and share links to meditations?

Could you write a regular blog with development tips? Run a

Facebook group with Live sessions? Offer competitions with a gift voucher as the prize?

Strategies for Off-Line Promotion

Off-line promotion is promotion that does not involve the internet.

Within your marketing budget, consider developing pamphlets, brochures and/or business cards that consistently portray your services, client message and brand. The client message is a succinct statement or slogan that represents you. Allocate a little time to research local notice boards, cafes, wellbeing centers, supermarkets, churches or community halls where you can display your flyers, a poster or business cards.

Most towns and cities have one or more business groups who meet regularly. Investigate the cost of joining one of these networks. Check out if they are actively promoting local business and if it seems worthwhile, join, attend their functions and network. Business organizations that have a joining fee will often offer one or two free 'guest attendances' before they require you to sign up. This will help you decide whether the organization is aligned to your business before you part with any fees.

Other Offline Ideas

- Research local fairs and business expos where you could promote your services.
- Offer to be the guest speaker at clubs and hobby groups. Explain how you work. A few short demonstrations build interest very quickly.
- There may be a local radio station who would love you to be their guest and field listener questions.
- Donate your time to charity. Offer a reading or a healing as a prize in a raffle for a charitable cause such as raising funds for cancer or helping a sick local child.
- Consider a stall or table at local markets. Take a friend with you so they can answer the public's questions as you work.

- Create good relationships with businesses that align with your work. Beyond the obvious businesses like spiritual shops, think about massage therapists, naturopaths, acupuncturists, chiropractors, health food shops and so on. Offer to demonstrate what you do so they have confidence in you. A free mini-session may convince them to recommend you.
- Take a small pile of their business cards and leave yours with them so you can cross-refer.
- Consider advertising in local newspapers and magazines. Be cautious. Gain feedback about the success rate of print advertising in your area before you invest.

Strategies for Online Promotion

Online promotional strategies use the internet. They have the potential to create a very large group of followers from which you will attract interested clients.

Your Website or Landing Page

A mistake I made in the early days of setting up a business was believing if I had a webpage, new clients would flock to it. I know now that was naïve, since how a website is set up and operated defines its success. A website is simply an online business card or brochure. It needs the ability to be found by search engines like Google and Chrome for it to meet its purpose. It won't be successful if you treat it like a puppy that you own for the joy of it.

Unless you are skilled in website creation and search engine optimization (SEO is how easily your site is found by those who are searching for what you do on the web), seek help from an expert. When I first started in business it cost thousands to get an active website that did its job. Today, however, it's much more cost effective and easier to do if you've got basic online skills.

Website software like WordPress or Weebly (and many others) make the job significantly easier today. At the time of publishing this book, there are services available that can build a basic site for very little in comparison to when I first started marketing online. Remember however, it's the SEO that is important in order for your website to be found by potential customers.

Organic and Paid Promotion on Facebook

Facebook offers a range of free and paid engagement models to build your client base and promote your business. The key to successfully using this very helpful and powerful social media platform for your business, is interaction. Get people talking to people and interacting with you. The information below focuses on attracting an audience of fans for Facebook; however, the strategies are also applicable to platforms such as LinkedIn and Instagram.

Organic Marketing on Facebook

Facebook provides many opportunities for organic marketing. Organic marketing strategies are without cost and can be extremely effective.

Rather than marketing through your personal profile, set up a Facebook business page that represents your brand. Build your client-base of followers on your business page. There is no cost to set up a Facebook business page, but to do so you must already have a personal page.

> *Facebook encourages interaction. It rewards you when you do a post that gets people talking and communicating with each other.*

The more comments you have on a post, the more you engage with your audience, the longer your post will stay in your newsfeed organically. Encourage viewers to comment on and like your posts. The first 24 hours is crucial. Your posts, whether featuring live videos or text, should align to a clear outcome that aligns with your marketing plan.

Live Videos

Video, and especially Live Stream video, are powerful strategies to build interest in you and your services. Going 'Live' on Facebook (and other social media platforms like YouTube and Instagram have their own versions of this) provides a cost-free opportunity for you to connect with people who relate to your message. When you provide variety in your content, or viewers learn that you offer free tips, inspiration and even regular mini-readings on your page, you'll gather a following of people who like, value and trust your messages.

You could record yourself Live as you offer free mini-psychic readings or a healing meditation on your business page at a set time and day each week.

With Live video, take the time to practice your presentation until you become confident with being in front of the video camera. You can do that by setting up a Private Group in Facebook. Only you or anyone you invite into that group will see your video. Spend a week or two going Live in that 'secret' group and then when you feel confident, go Live on your business page. You can go to my Facebook business page - The Academy of Spiritual Practice - for examples of Live video streams I have presented.

Every Live video should work towards an outcome and be logically structured. Here is an example of how to structure a Live video.

- An introduction (Introduce yourself, your topic, who it's for and what's in it for them.)
- Content (Depending on the length of the video keep the content of each video to one topic. Make no more than three points about that topic, and fewer if the Live is shorter.)

- Provide a call to action (What they need to do next, e.g. "Show me you're enjoying this by commenting below," or "If you like what you've heard, make sure you follow me to get notified when I'm Live," or "Comment below if you'd like my free x, y or z.")
- Conclusion (End your video with your consistent brand message, personal name and business name.)

Be aware that at the time of writing this book, Facebook algorithms take three minutes or more for their bots to find you an audience that might want to see your Live. So, mix up the length of your Live Videos, but aim for a little over three minutes on average. This means Facebook's programs can help your video reach the best audience.

Be engaging and give a generous amount of relevant free content. This includes specific information about what you do as well as helpful general information about your area of expertise.

> Be aware that at the time of writing this book, Facebook algorithms take three minutes or more for their bots to find you an audience that might want to see your Live. So, mix up the length of your Live Videos, but aim for a little over three minutes on average. This means Facebook's programs can help your video reach the best audience.

Don't come across as 'hard sell'. Provide information and then tell people how they can learn more. Keep your content and tone positive. If you want to build a large audience organically (which means free marketing) you need to consider lots of short live videos that are saved on your page. You can then download them and use them for other purposes too. Re-purposing content makes your marketing job easier. Translate the video to text, edit it into a blog, add it to your website and share the link with Facebook and other social media platforms.

Be warm, friendly and confident. Never criticize another person or include negative content. When your audience trusts you and thinks what you offer is both important to them and of value, you will organically build a fan base.

Always invite viewers to 'like' and/or comment on your posts and Live stream videos and any offer it contains. Invite them to message you privately if they would like to discuss personal challenges or have a reading or other service.

Whether you are writing a post or posting a video, write a new comment and tag every person who responds to your post. At the time of writing this chapter, commenting back is more effective than just clicking 'reply'.

Invite friends to share your post/video. Keep the interaction going as long as you can. Share your video across all your pages, even in groups you have joined, providing you have permission to do so.

Your aim is to be of service, just as it is in your intuitive practice. Build desire in your followers and viewers by being of service to them with valid, interesting, inspiring, educational or motivational content. Be yourself. Be authentic. Viewers sense a fraud. Be upfront, and you'll build loyal followers that like, value and trust what you do. Every three or four posts on your page, remember to invite your audience to connect further with you by explaining how they can book a service or take up an offer. If you do the hard sell for your business in every post, followers will not follow you. Remember, people don't like to be sold to, but they do like to buy when it feels right for them.

When you are authentically of service to your audience, and you provide ways for them to contact you without the hard sell, you attract the right audience who want to know how you can help them more.

Be very aware of Facebook's guidelines and rules. Never market to someone who has not requested the information on Facebook. Never market in Messenger to someone who is not your friend and hasn't asked for your service or product. Facebook programs detect unsolicited marketing and may block your account. Request that anyone who would like more information sends you a message or requests it on your post.

Always make sure any landing pages (webpages) you link to are positive in nature, and relevant to the offer you have made. You may have your account blocked if you breach Facebook's ethical guidelines. If you share links to your website or landing page, these also need to have your privacy policy and terms of service. Without them, Facebook will not approve your boosted post or advertisement.

If you plan to invest money to boost a post, make sure the post has organic engagement first. Remember, Facebook is more likely to show posts on the newsfeed organically, when people are engaging in the post.

Facebook Groups

Whether you establish a public group or a closed group, Facebook groups offer an excellent opportunity to build targeted followers at no cost. The key to gain maximum reach, is to over-deliver great content to your members - content that gets them talking to each other. Once a group has a certain number of members, and has very active members communicating with each other, Facebook algorithms will organically show the group to others who have an interest in that topic.

If you want to build a loyal following of potential clients on social media, consider starting a public or closed Facebook group and share healing tips and spiritual information.

You could also offer helpful tips to your social media followers in the form of a lead magnet. A lead magnet is a free PDF, discount, or 'giveaway' with valuable content that you offer in exchange for their email address. Growing an email subscribers' list, and nurturing them over time with further helpful content, ensures you no longer only rely on one way of staying in contact with your followers.

Paid Marketing on Facebook

In addition to organic strategies, you can run paid-marketing campaigns on Facebook. Skillful marketing campaigns can be very effective; however, I recommend you research well and start with small budgets as you learn how to run ad campaigns.

Facebook provides excellent training programs in how to write and develop advertising campaigns. Your success in paid Facebook marketing depends on how skillfully you target your audience and craft your ads within your budget. Undertaking the training provided by Facebook is recommended to improve the success rate and the value you receive for investment. You might also consider engaging a professional digital marketer to develop and run campaigns so that you can compare your results.

Other Online Social Media Platforms

In addition to Facebook, other platforms such as Twitter and Instagram each target different demographics. I suggest researching the platform that your ideal client uses most frequently, then investing the time to become skilled at that platform. Do this before spreading your time, energy and potential budget too thinly. Begin with one social media platform. Build your audience there first.

Network with other professional practitioners on LinkedIn. LinkedIn allows you to maintain an active professional profile and participate in discussions that keep you immersed in your industry. It's a great way to stay up-to-date with what other professionals in your field are offering.

While the business creation and marketing strategies suggested cannot cover the entirety of such a large topic, you have a starting point from which to investigate and move forward.

Moving forward is an apt theme as we consider everything I have covered in this book. I have revealed all 8 Keys to intuitive excellence and what you do with those keys, is now your choice.

> Remember the words of Spirit, which were so clearly placed in my mind:
> *'A key has little value, until you put it in a lock and turn it.'*

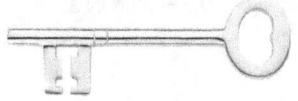

CHAPTER 9

NEW BEGINNINGS

In bringing the journey of this book to a conclusion, I know that the journey of your intuitive gifts continues.

An ending is like a beginning. Each evolves from a point that is seldom planned, but emerges nevertheless, to redirect the flow of our lives. Sometimes there is a gentle fork in the road, a choice between paths that wind their way through territory unknown. Other times we find ourselves on the edge of a cliff, with the wind at our back and nothing but sky before us, contemplating a leap of faith.

Like The Fool in the Tarot, we step into nothingness, relying on alchemy and the whisperings of our soul, to save us - a soul that reminds us we are eternal, loving beings for whom death is not a possibility.

We are human in form, yet Light at our core. Being spiritual is the most natural thing we know.

We learn, grow and face our challenges with courage, resilience and compassion. We do not fail. We do not deny who we are. Our soul is our compass and Spirit, our guide. The process may not be easy, but then again, a catalyst for change is seldom comfortable.

Paul Cavanough discovered for himself how uncomfortable an unplanned life-change can be early in 2018. Until that time, Paul had been happy to have horticulture as his profession and his intuitive gifts as a passion; however, a serious back injury suddenly removed the option of physical work. Paul realized that working in horticulture was no longer possible, and yet he had a young family to support.

A humble, quietly spoken man with a powerful intuitive gift, Paul kindly allowed me to share with you his experience of transitioning his intuitive gifts from a passion to his profession.

My relationship with Paul's spiritual growth has spanned 12 years. Our spiritual journeys have led us to become trusted friends. For some years Paul sat in my home meditation circle, attended the church where I was a spiritualist minister and participated in spiritual development workshops I facilitated. I have mentored and encouraged him through some tough experiences, and it is wonderful for me to see him working professionally with his gift.

Paul honored me when he accepted the invitation to share his story by saying that I was a light in his journey and a large part of the reason he is working professionally today. Paul also said, *"I started behind the 8-ball. I was low in confidence. It was your structured teaching, your gentle truth and your belief in your message that defined my gift."*

Paul's Story
CASE STUDY

Finances became tight for Paul and his family after a back injury caused him to lose his principal means of income. This forced Paul to assess his life.

He already had a close relationship with his spiritual guides and knew he had a strong intuitive and healing gift. Taking a leap of faith, Paul decided to dedicate himself to working with his gifts from a compassionate heart. Even so, Paul reports that the way his journey unfolded was like a series of steps or terraces, rather than following a smooth path. It wasn't as simple as just putting one foot in front of another. Lessons had to be stabilized and accepted before the next level, the next opportunity for growth, presented itself. Paul had to be personally ready and also willing to receive the guidance he was offered, and this took time.

Since he transitioned to full-time spiritual work, Paul has developed three key services and established his business, *Energy Well*.

1. He has a room in a spiritual shop, from which he offers intuitive readings.
2. He has a dedicated room in his home where he provides intuitively guided energy healings and readings.
3. He works online as a psychic reader for an international company, having passed the stringent skills-tests required by this company for employment.

> I asked Paul if he would share the practical steps he follows that help him work effectively. He revealed that in the past twelve years he has worked on himself extensively and cleaned up his lifestyle. Paul also understands that his gift must be respected and never abused by ego.
>
> Maintaining clear, high energy is essential before and during his readings and healings. Every morning Paul uses a breath technique to ground himself with his body, before lifting his energy towards the spirit world.
>
> He then completes a color meditation that energizes and clears his chakras. He added that sometimes his energy vibrates so fast he feels almost transparent. Paul requests protection from all negativity through prayer and sets a strong intention to be a channel for compassion. He allows the intuitive information he receives to pass through him uncensored, rather than interjecting with personal opinions. Paul always clears his environment with light after working and does the same for himself during his shower.

Paul says, *"In the beginning of 2018 I was given a message in the middle of the night by my guides. After working part-time with my gifts until then, they urged me to offer psychic readings online."*

This message gave Paul the courage to read for strangers all over the world. Even he is stunned by the insights that come to him, or rather, through him.

Paul's preparation for a day's intuitive work takes between forty-five and fifty minutes. He is meticulous because the quality of his intuitive insights depends on his clarity as a channel for his guides and his intuition.

Working online from home offers Paul flexibility and the opportunity to spend time with his family. He feels gratitude for the work he performs through his gift. He backs himself because he knows that his gift is real, and his clients realize it very quickly.

Paul understands and uses the keys outlined in this book, because we have discussed them together over many years.

- He has personally confronted and transformed himself as part of his journey. He has undergone the alchemy of his own empowerment.
- He builds and maintains a clear energy field, using intention and protection every day.
- He knows how to lift and blend energies with his client and his guides to sustain the best connections for each intention.
- His evidence is relevant, practical, accurate and he delivers his message with compassion.
- Life has taught Paul that he needs to take care of himself. The vessel that is his body needs to be cared for. This has been a large lesson for him.
- Paul has established a full-time profession as an intuitive reader and healer, having finally transitioned his passion into his profession.

So, where are you right now, I wonder?

Are you standing before a fork in the road, perhaps finding the decision quite natural, or are you contemplating stepping off that cliff and taking a leap of faith? You may be in neither of these places, or perhaps you have been there before.

Your intuitive gifts ignite a passion within you, and while all passions are personal, do you feel the calling to offer more? Does your soul niggle you to take that leap of faith and work with your intuitive gifts?

Were you, like I was, born for this?

This book did not set out to teach you to become intuitive or learn a new craft. Its purpose is to polish the gems you already hold so they shine more brightly.

You now have eight keys to unlock the intuitive excellence within you. What has happened for you as you shared the journey of my book?

> These are my hopes for you.
>
> - You have stepped into your confidence and learned to build, sustain and protect your energy. The world feels less overwhelming. You have enriched your personal database and understand that living a full and satisfying life provides you with the experiences that create your evidence.
>
> - You know how to direct your energy according to the connections you need. Being the 'Key-Master,' you understand that your focus and attention open the spiritual channels between worlds. You blend energies with your client and your spiritual helpers to enhance your intuition and you communicate your messages sensitively and skillfully within a professional process.
>
> - You are the professional in thought and deed. A high level of ethics underpins your practice and you care for yourself as well as others. You are the instrument of your gift, and you respect that.
>
> - Whether you establish a professional practice or just practice like a professional, you have mastered the keys to excellence.

If there was one special 'jewel' that the 8 Keys in this book might have revealed, it is this:

Remember always to set an empowered intention with compassion and healing at its core. Your intention shines into the spiritual worlds. When you signal you want to help, heal and uplift, no matter your gift, your loving spiritual guides will always support you.

Blessings and Light

Michelle

ACKNOWLEDGMENTS

With gratitude, I wish to acknowledge the following people who have supported me during the writing, editing and publication of this book:

My husband, John Noble, and children Abigail and Cameron, for their steadfast love and faith in my abilities.

Maggie Wilde for her outstanding expertise and encouragement as a mentor, an editor, a contributor and publisher.

Trish Walker, for her kindness, gentle coaching, proof-reading and dedication to the project.

Kathryn Keenan ('Katy-K') for her support and for writing the foreword for my book amid a very busy professional life.

Cathy Rodwell for designing the graphic images in the text.

Julie Love, Julie-Ann Bradwyn, Suzanne Heggie and Aithne Mayes - my 4 wise friends - for inspiration, motivation and the sanity of great friendship.

Jan Shaw for her kind assistance with photos.

The psychics, healers and mediums who contributed their professional tips and experiences throughout the book. You will meet them in the 'Contributors' section at the end of the book.

The real people with real-life stories whose experiences inspired case-studies throughout this book (some names have been changed for privacy reasons). I offer gratitude to you that our paths crossed, your stories now assist others to refine their intuitive gifts.

MEET THE CONTRIBUTORS

Each of the following contributors works professionally as a psychic, medium and/or healer, many of them internationally. I thank them for sharing their tips, expertise or personal story. Their real-life experiences add to the book's authenticity and worth.

Writer of the Foreword: Kathryn Keenan - 'Katy-K'

'Katy-K' is an Australian born psychic medium and spiritual development teacher who travels and works Internationally. Katy is the creator of the very popular 'The Modern Oracle' deck that was published in 2015 and 'The Modern Oracle of Essential Oils' deck that was published in 2019. She also holds the privilege of being awarded the International Psychics Directory '2015 Psychic People's Choice Award.'

Katy comes from a long line of mediums and psychics. She attended The Arthur Findlay College in England for more than 10 years, as well as studying under many renowned psychics and mediums internationally.

Katy is the founder of the 'KTK Spiritual Development Academy' and she has made it her mission to teach easier ways to develop your intuitive gifts, modernizing the way spiritual development is taught through her online courses and meditations. Katy is very proud of the fact that she has coached and produced many psychics through one-on-one coaching and mentoring, who have then gone on to open their own practice. You can access Katy's 'Modern Oracle' decks, online courses, meditations and coaching sessions at her website

www.katy-k.com

MEET THE CONTRIBUTORS

Julie-Ann Bradwyn

Julie-Ann Bradwyn had a corporate background but was always highly intuitive, with her work and decisions guided by her 'knowings'. After joining a spiritual church and expanding her psychic senses, she felt a pull towards healing and mediumship. She found direct communication with Spirit was a natural gift and offering platform demonstrations is her passion. Julie-Ann now works as a Reiki Master and psychic medium, offering workshops, healings, private sittings and platform demonstrations.

You can connect with Julie-Ann on her Facebook Page 'Jewel Connections Psychic Medium'

https://www.facebook.com/jewelconnections/

Sunny Burgess

Spirit Listener. B.A (Design). H.N.D (Business Economics). B.Ed. (1st class honors).

Sunny Burgess has been working as a trance medium for 30 years. His gifts came from an early age, when he experienced chronic somnambulism (sleep walking trances) from 4 years to the age of 25, after which he entered into spiritualism and developed his gift.

Sunny's demonstrations of mediumship in Australia attract audiences of over 500 attendees, and they are often sold out. Videos of some of these public shows, together with rare footage of his trance work in private red light seances, can be viewed on his website www.sunnyspirit.net

Paul Cavanough

Paul Cavanough is an international psychic medium based on the Sunshine Coast in Queensland, Australia. He is the father of 3 children, 2 dogs and 4 fish. He is an avid hiker, motorcycle rider and ocean swimmer, all of which give him the freedom and solitude he enjoys. Paul is also a qualified Reiki Master and has completed many short courses in different healing modalities. His passion is to see people free of internal suffering in order to attain contentment with self.

Paul works with people around the world on a daily basis and can be contacted at https://www.facebook.com/EnergyWellAus/

Marco Della Valle

Marco Della Valle is an international psychic medium who conducts both psychic and mediumship readings, along with training and educating people on how to develop their own abilities.

With an international clientele, Marco utilizes his senses of clairvoyance, clairaudience and clairsentience to connect and deliver messages from the spirit world with evidence.

Having written a regular monthly column for an Australian magazine, along with being featured on several radio programs, Marco's aim is to give comfort to his clients and those he meets.

Connect with Marco on his website: www.marcodellavalle.com

MEET THE CONTRIBUTORS

Cathy Rodwell

Cathy Rodwell (MEd) is an artist and healer whose unique therapy supports the bonding of soul fragments when past traumas may have caused energy to become scattered. She also assists in enabling deep personal experiences and communication for her clients with loved ones in spirit.

Connect with Cathy at
www.CathyRodwell.com

Kathryn Simeon

Kathryn Simeon is an experienced psychic medium, spiritual teacher and mentor who works face to face and online.

Her psychic readings and spiritual mentoring programs uplift her clients through her caring nature, accurate insights and practical skills-training. Kath often uses Tarot cards to connect with her client's questions. She loves teaching others what she has learned through her own professional experience. Kath also receives direct messages from loved ones in spirit. You can connect with Kathryn on her Facebook Page

www.facebook.com/KathPsychicClairvoyant/

Maggie Wilde - The Potentialist

Maggie is the Founder of Mind Potential Academy and Mind Potential Publishing. She is a 10-time award winning author and publisher and her unique C P R Brain Training Model™ is taught to Wellness Practitioners worldwide.

Maggie is a Mentor and Publisher to Healthcare Practitioners, enabling their businesses and profiles to expand globally. She and her clients are regularly featured in local, national and international media including: Ch 7 Sunrise, Ch 9 A Current Affair, The Daily Edition. CW6 San Diego Living, Good Morning New Mexico, Law of Attraction Radio (Los Angeles), Conscious Living TV and more.

www.thepotentialist.com
https://facebook.com/MaggieWildeAuthor

FURTHER READING

Alexander, Eben DR. *Proof of Heaven: A Neurosurgeon's Journey into the Afterlife.* Simon & Schuster US, 2012.

Bolzicevic-Mewes, Debbie. *The Reluctant Psychic: A Psychic Mediums Journey and Tips to Your Own Psychic Development.* Universal Lifepsycle, Sunshine Coast, QLD, Australia, 2010.

Cayce, Edgar. *The Psychic Senses: How to Awaken Your Sixth Sense to Solve Life's Problems and Seize Opportunities.* A.R.E. Press, Virginia Beach, 2006.

Doidge, Norman. *The Brain That Changes Itself: Stories of Personal Triumph from the Frontiers of Brain Science.* Penguin Group, New York, 2007.

Dyer, Wayne W DR. *Real Magic: Creating Miracles In Everyday Life.* Harper Collins, Sydney, Australia, 1992.

Henry, Tyler, *Between Two Worlds. Lessons From The Other Side*, Gallery Books, U.S, 2017.

Holland, John. *The Spirit Whisperer: Chronicles Of A Medium.* Hay House Inc, US, 2010.

Leaf, Caroline. *Who Switched Off My Brain? Controlling Toxic Thoughts and Emotions.* Grand Rapids, Baker Books, 2007.

Millman, Dan. *The Life You Were Born To Live: A Guide To Finding Your Life Purpose.* HJ Kramer and New World Library, CA, 1993.

Newton, Michael PH.D. *Journey of Souls: Case Studies of Life Between Lives.* Llewellyn Publications, Minnesota, 1994.

Ring, Kenneth PH.D. *Lessons From The Light: What we can learn from the near-death experience.* Moment Point Press, Massachusetts, 2006.

Robinson, Michelle. *I'm Positive! Program Your Thoughts and*

Feelings to Create a Positive Life. Tablo, Australia, 2019.

Robinson, Michelle. *Karma Couples: A Spiritual Self-Help Guide for Troubled Karmic Relationships.* Tablo, Australia, 2019.

Roman, Sanaya and Packer Duane. *Opening To Channel: How To Connect With Your Guide.* HJ Kramer, CA, 1987.

Seaman, Judith. *Trance Mediumship.* SDU Publications, UK, 2008.

Stockwell, Tony. *Embracing Eternity.* Hodder & Stoughton, U.K, 2006.

Smith, Gordon. *Developing Mediumship.* Hay House, UK, 2009.

Smith, Peter. Quantam Consciousness: *Expanding Your Personal Universe.* The Consciousness Collective, Warrandyte, Australia, 2015.

Tolle, Eckhart. *The Power Of Now: A Guide To Spiritual Enlightenment.* Hodder Australia, Sydney, 1999.

Weiss, Brian L. M.D. *Many Lives, Many Masters: The True Story of a Prominent Psychiatrist, His Young Patient, and the Past-Life Therapy That Changed Both Their Lives.* Simon & Schuster, New York, 1988.

Wilde, Maggie. *Unleashed: How to Embrace Who You Are and Empower Yourself to Reach Your Potential - Fast!* Black Card Books, Canada.

Williams, Lisa. *Life Among The Dead.* Simon & Schuster, New York, 2008.

Website

The International Institute for Complementary Therapists, available at www.myiict.com

TESTIMONIALS

"Michelle's integrity and dedication to the healing arts is beyond measure. I have found her inspirational trance control to be equally outstanding: words beyond platitude and replete with the cosmic dust of spiritual truth to nourish the spiritual seeker of the modern world."

Sunny Burgess, Spirit Listener, Medium

"Michelle has a wealth of knowledge in all things esoteric. Combined with her academic background she brings an informative and structured experience to all who are lucky enough to receive her teaching. She is a practical gift to an undefined industry."

Paul Cavanough, Psychic Medium

"Michelle has a warm and caring nature which draws people to her. Her spiritual insightfulness, her intuitive abilities, plus her gentle manner allow people to feel safe and secure in her presence."

Suzanne Heggie, attendee of Michelle's spiritual group.

"Michelle is an amazing mentor and spiritual teacher. I have also had several readings from Michelle, and I am blown away by her accuracy, every time. She is honest, accurate, and always reads from the heart."

Kathryn Simeon, Psychic Medium

ABOUT THE AUTHOR

Michelle Robinson

B.A., Dip. ED., Bach. Couns., Cert Past Life and Soul Regression, Dip. CH.

Michelle comes from a mainstream background; however, using her intuitive gifts is both her passion and profession. She is a qualified teacher, counselor and hypnotherapist with twenty years' experience working with adults and teenagers. She is also an intuitive healer, a trance medium and psychic.

Michelle has studied extensively with Australian and international mediums, psychics and healers. She facilitates groups and mentors individuals both face to face and online. Topics include Inspired Trance, Trance Healing, Reiki, Development of Psychic and Mediumship Skills, Past Life Exploration and Personal Empowerment. She has a practical approach to spirituality, knowing it is important to stay grounded and authentic. Trance is one of her special gifts, during which she receives channeled wisdom from a team of spiritual guides.

In 2019 Michelle and husband, John Noble established 'The Academy of Spiritual Practice.' The Academy's vision is to share the inspiration of Spirit by offering Michelle's spiritual development programs, meditations and authored works online.

Michelle is a published author. Previous titles include:

'I'm Positive!' Program Your Thoughts and Feelings to Create a Positive Life.'

'Karma Couples - A Spiritual Self-Help Guide for Troubled Karmic Relationships'

These works are published by Tablo and available on Amazon, Kindle and other platforms.

EXISTING WORKS BY MICHELLE ROBINSON

'I'm Positive! Program Your Thoughts and Feelings to Create a Positive Life.'

Packed full of helpful strategies and information, *'I'm Positive'* is your guide to creating an energized, positive life. More than twenty years of experience as a counselor and hypnotherapist in professional practice led Michelle to write this book.

'I'm Positive!' helps you let go of unhelpful thought patterns, emotional hurts and outdated beliefs so you feel confident, optimistic and in control of your choices. If you have been undermining your own achievements or impacted by the negativity of others, this book shows you how to steer your life in the right direction.

Program your mind so that positive thoughts and feelings are your natural default.

'Karma Couples - A Spiritual Self-Help Guide for Troubled Karmic Relationships'

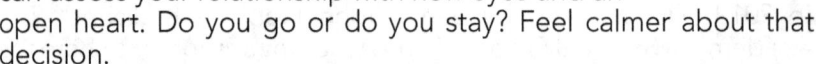

'Karma Couples' is a spiritual self-help book for partners in a troubled relationship.

It helps you recognize the soul contracts and soul lessons you developed with your partner before you incarnated on Earth. From here, you can assess your relationship with new eyes and an open heart. Do you go or do you stay? Feel calmer about that decision.

'Karma Couples' assists you release pain, blame and guilt, focusing you instead on the loving intention behind your union and the higher plan guiding your life.

You can find Michelle's books on Amazon, Kindle and other major publishing platforms in hard cover and electronic format.

 You can download it HERE.
www.yourintuitivegiftsatwork.com/freeaudios

www.ingramcontent.com/pod-product-compliance
Lightning Source LLC
Chambersburg PA
CBHW071629080526
44588CB00010B/1327